On Constance

Karin Konoval

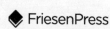 FriesenPress

One Printers Way
Altona, MB R0G 0B0
Canada

www.friesenpress.com

ISBN
978-1-03-915984-6 (Hardcover)
978-1-03-915983-9 (Paperback)
978-1-03-915985-3 (eBook)

1. TRAVEL, ESSAYS & TRAVELOGUES

Distributed to the trade by The Ingram Book Company

One

Readying

In April 2013, I boarded a train in Seattle heading for New Orleans. There, I'd be joining cast and crew for the filming of the second in a trilogy of films. Everyone else was flying down. At the time, I didn't fly. So, the train. This story isn't about the film, though the fact that I was playing a mature male orangutan in it laid the path, in a way, for how my personal journey beyond the work would unfold.

I'd always wanted to go to New Orleans. I can't remember why. It wasn't simply to experience the music and food, to walk Bourbon Street or go to Mardi Gras, or even to step into the history. It was something less nameable, perhaps just a sense or wish that it might be a magical place?

Playing a mature male orangutan is a unique undertaking, aside from the obvious that it's a character of a different species and gender from my own. It seems to require a solitude beyond the work itself. It's true that in the wild they are largely solitary individuals, but I've played many solitary human characters that I step away from when wrap for the day is called on a film set or the curtain comes down on a stage performance. I value the return to self, I don't like to carry characters in my mind and energy twenty-four hours a day. But playing an orangutan . . . this was different.

Through the filming of the first movie in the trilogy in Vancouver, I'd felt very much alone, and lonely, until I realized: it came with the gig. Inhabiting the stillness and keen watchfulness of this orangutan character not only kept me in a different energetic space from the actors who were playing chimpanzees and gorillas, but it called on me to stay in that place. Full time. I still chatted with colleagues over lunch or at the craft services table, still enjoyed the people in my regular life, but with a part of me anchored in orangutan solitude for the duration of filming. Seeing the world around me differently, even. By the end of the first shoot, I finally relaxed and accepted this. Inside the watching, in fact, I didn't feel lonely at all. When the second film was coming up, for months before shooting began, I was readying my body for the physical challenges. I was also readying myself to step back into that place of watchful solitude. This time I would embrace it from the start, let it lead me.

I left home in Vancouver, B.C., for Seattle on a sunny day in April. I had with me a single large suitcase, filled with just the essentials I felt I'd need for the next four months: the script in its massive binder, light clothing for what I'd been warned would be a sweltering New Orleans summer, some art supplies for my painting and drawing hobby, and four hula hoops—two smaller arm hoops and two larger collapsible ones. As part of my physical training for the film, besides yoga and weight lifting in the gym, and quadrupedal walking and running on arm stilts in the park near home, I'd recently taken up hula hooping. I'm not sure how much it contributed to orangutan training, beyond a certain core workout and a different way to build arm strength. Mostly I just liked it. The feeling of the hoops circling on my arms and body, the fluidity of movement (when I wasn't dropping them, which I often was), the sort of inward quiet spiraling place they sometimes took me to. They made me laugh, at how inept I was. I doubted I'd ever be a good hooper, which didn't bother me in the slightest. They were fun.

The only other things I brought were a camera and a notebook and pen. If I was going to be alone on this journey, I would watch and photograph and write. I wondered: in my personal time away from work, where would New Orleans lead me? What story would fill my notebook?

Before catching the train in Seattle, I went to the zoo. I wanted to say a farewell to dear human friends who worked there, and the five orangutans they cared for. This would be the longest time I'd be away from them since I'd begun to visit regularly, two years earlier. Every six or eight weeks at most, at least three full days per visit, and already at the two-year mark, what I'd seen and experienced with this orangutan family could fill a book. One of the orangutans, Towan, had been my inspiration for the role I was playing. His depth and quietude, keen observance and strength of spirit, had not only given me the key to the character but to think of Towan at any point, on set or off, anchored me instantly. A constant friend across the ether, as it were, who I felt understood what I was doing better than anyone. As only a mature male orangutan could.

I said a brief hello to four of the orangutans—Melati, Chinta, Bela and Heran. Melati and I generally spent several hours a day together during my visits, painting, me on one side of the window with paper and paint, her on the other side choosing colors and banging on the window when she wished me to change them. As I arrived, she came right to the window, ready for painting to begin. When I didn't instantly get to it, she was incensed. She pounded the window with her fist and pointed for me to sit down. My stomach sank as I shook my head no, blew her a kiss, and slipped away. The coming absence would be close to four months. I already missed her, not even having left yet.

I was taken for a rare private visit with Towan. As always, I put on a face mask, sterilized my shoes on a mat, then was led through a door to the back area of the indoor habitat. It was a lovely day, and Towan was outside in the trees. He came when called, and right to the mesh to visit. We looked into each other. My keeper friend explained to him, in words, that I was going away on a long trip. I made a circling gesture with my index fingers to suggest how long it would be before I came back. I'd gotten into the habit of this pidgin sign language with the orangutans when leaving at any point, whether for a bathroom break or lunch or at the end of a visit, to let them know when I'd return. A two-finger gesture from my eyes to theirs to say "see you," then the circling index fingers to suggest a space of time, followed by two fingers up for two minutes, meaning a short break, or a bite of invisible food to suggest I was just leaving for lunch, or, at the very end of a three-day visit, a "bye-bye" wave to let them know it would be weeks before I'd be back. Who could say if they understood? Today as I write this, nine years later and a lot more water under the bridge between us, I am certain they do.

So I circled and circled my index fingers round each other to Towan, and stretched my hands wide to increase the distance between them, as I told him in words the great length of time I'd be away, how far away I was going, and how much I would miss him. I asked if he'd give me a gift. I asked this in words, from behind my mask, no gesture. I wasn't expecting an actual thing, more asking for his blessing in a way. Towan stared into me for a long beat, then reached behind himself and fiddled with something. He held it up. A piece of straw. My friend nodded that he could give it to me. Towan passed it carefully through the mesh. I put it in the shirt pocket over my heart and pressed my hand to the pocket, thanking him. One more long beat of looking into each other, then the "bye-bye" wave, and I headed for the train. With my big suitcase holding the script, summer clothing, art supplies, and hula hoops . . . my camera and notebook and pen at the ready for the journey to begin.

Two

Getting There

MONDAY, APRIL 29. OUR sleeping car attendant on the Empire Builder to Chicago is Stan. He's worked the rails for thirty-eight years and will retire in "three more trips!" He grins and holds up three fingers. For the next forty-four hours, more than half the width of the country and at every station stop along the way, Stan will be greeted by platform conductors, baggage cart drivers, and just about every Amtrak employee we meet, "three more trips, Stan!" And a responding three finger salute. Stan is liked by everyone and a fountain of information on everything from the inner workings of computers to the history of the Roman Empire.

In the dining car, rocking through eastern Washington: my dinner companions are a couple who met, married, and bought a house on three Friday the thirteenths. They're on a forty-five-day train journey across America to celebrate the husband's sixtieth birthday. They tell me to order my steak medium, my potato well done, and that there will be trees coming up on our journey that look like they're dancing over the ground in skirts.

Midnight, Spokane, Washington. At the station, the Kochi Teriyaki Gift Shop and Cafeteria is still serving. Besides food you can choose from a selection of gifts displayed on shelves in the unrefrigerated cooler case: a wooden chess board, a Disney Princess hat-and-glove set, four toy bomber jets in a box, a twelve-piece cookware ensemble for kids, an AM/FM mini radio, a toy Honda racing motorcycle, a clear carrying case the size and shape of a cake containing one small comb, one small mirror and two bangle bracelets, a box of tiny racing cars with parking garage, and a set of six miniature geishas posing in various positions of their dance.

❖ ❖ ❖

Tuesday, April 30. Eight a.m., just past Whitefish, Montana. The Empire Builder climbs into Glacier National Park and a blizzard of snow. In the observation car I meet Annette, who's going home to Shelby. It's a brown, scrubby land she tells me,

"There's nothing there."

She longs for the green and trees of Leavenworth where she grew up. Her husband Michael joins us, a big man with a massive handshake who drives truckloads of apples. Our train stops in the snow to wait for a freight train to pass. Michael spots something outside the window, blinking in a half-frozen pond.

"See, there! Like two little headlights going on and off again."

It takes me several minutes to spot it: the tiniest frog, clinging to a branch just below the pond's surface. Only its eyes are visible, blink-blinking, the water rippling out in circles with each blink. When the train gets going again, we climb further into the mountains, then descend to the prairie floor. It is white, white, white forever, all snow and white sky. I photograph landscape for hours, riveted by the same nothingness Annette longs to escape.

Somewhere between Shelby and Havre I go for lunch in the dining car. There's a skinny older gentleman with buck teeth, baggy trousers, and a backpack who I've seen pacing the station platform on fresh air breaks. He sits down across from me. He's always grinning, seems delighted with the ride. But when I smile at him, he looks down and won't meet my eyes again for the rest of lunch.

A man and woman join us. They look like a farm couple, the man in dirty work boots. No one offers names. Instead, we ask each other where we've come from, where we're heading. The grinning older gentleman says he left New York a month ago by ship to Europe, then somehow to Asia and across it, then by ship to Vancouver from Japan. I've noticed that one of his forearms is covered with psoriasis wounds, he looks down and presses at them as he speaks.

"Did you go to Downton Abbey?" asks the fellow in dirty work boots, who sits beside me. "That's what I'd go to see. I just love that show."

The grinning older gentleman stops grinning. "No!" he barks. He looks down and digs into his spaghetti and meatballs, doesn't say another word to us.

Across the aisle a child waves his sock monkey at me. I wave back.

At Havre, Montana, the sign on the Oxford Sports Bar opposite the station reads "Spending Money Relieves Stress." I hear Stan, our sleeping car attendant, and a new conductor discussing the floods and rerouting ahead. They hope that plan B for our route isn't flooded now too. Eastern Montana rolls by . . . dry, scrubby, few trees, grain fields, a peek of sun between clouds. Just before North Dakota I decide to have a shower, an adventurous undertaking on a moving train. There's an announcement over the intercom: a little boy has lost his sock monkey and needs it back.

I have dinner again with the couple who met, married, and bought a house on three Friday the thirteenths. We're joined by a woman who fights back tears. Her husband just left her, she tells us, and she's on her way to break the news to her son in college. Once she was a dental hygienist, now with her marriage gone and kids grown she has no idea what comes next.

"I don't know what to do with myself. What do you think?" A well-dressed pretty woman, she searches our faces.

Oil rigs, oil rigs, hay bales, oil rigs . . . at Minot, North Dakota, there's a fresh air break. The older gentleman with buck teeth, baggy trousers, and a backpack paces the platform, checking his watch. The little boy who lost his sock monkey has a new teddy bear. The woman who lost her husband hurries into the station to find a way to fax a court order. She comes back shaking her head, No. We all get back on board and the Empire Builder rolls into the night, heading off course now to avoid the floods.

❖　❖　❖

Wednesday, May 1. Our train keeps to schedule and makes it past the floods, arriving early in Saint Paul where it's bleak and cold and pouring rain. I have breakfast with Eunice from Wisconsin and Kevin from Chicago. Kevin tells us of playing music in Memphis, driving to Sacramento, and seeing whales in the Pacific. He tells how he explains climate differences to his kids: that the world is a bowl and you travel over it like this—he shows us with his hand—so you can move from one climate to another in such a short distance.

He tells of other amazing things he's explained to his kids. Like, the giants who once roamed the earth and still do now. They are the "nel-phins," he says, victims of a grand cover-up conspiracy, beings who are nine to fifteen feet tall and have done such things as try out for the NBA and get rejected, then disappear, so you never hear of them again. He tells of a scientist who found the portal to the center of the earth, went there and visited, came back out and quit his job as a scientist because he had no way to explain this, and from then on, believed in God.

I'm watching Eunice's face over her porridge as Kevin speaks. She is as tidy and put together as her name sounds, and the pleasant smile she brought to breakfast has frozen in place.

I retreat to my warm room and a favorite blanket I'm so glad I brought, it's like a little home in here. Then, outside my window: the first glimpse of the Mississippi River rolling by.

My lunch companions are a psychologist and her son. He's won the Regional Bible Knowledge Championship, and they're on their way to the nationals in New York. He's fourteen, a huge kid—could be one of Kevin's "nelphins." He opens two butter pats and mashes them on top of his dinner roll. His mother suggests he use a knife to cut the roll and spread the butter inside, but he looks confused. She orders two kids' meals for him—chicken fingers and fries and a cheese pizza—and gives him her own dinner roll to tide him over until the food comes. When the plates arrive there's a splotch of grease on one of them, which upsets him.

"I'm sorry," says his mother. "I didn't know that would be there." She wipes the plate clean. She keeps speaking gently to him, suggesting how to eat his meal. Her voice seems to soothe him.

The boy tells me what it will be like to be on a stage in front of hundreds of people answering questions about the Bible, how exciting if he wins the trip to Israel, how he plays the clarinet, how he loves basketball. His mother tells of how she was an extra in a movie once, and wore a red dress. She got picked to jump down from a box to greet the rock-and-roll star of the movie, and did this over and over for a full day. The scene wound up on the cutting room floor but it was the highlight of her youth, she says.

Back in my room the window is warm to the touch for the first time since we left Seattle. Milwaukee . . . a big sign for Miller Beer . . . Stan comes to make up my room one last time before we arrive in Chicago. It takes almost an hour because we keep coming up with one more thing to talk about before we say goodbye.

The train station in Chicago is grimy and loud, packed with people. It's surprisingly unsettling to be spit out into the throngs after the past forty-four hours in my little home of a room on the Empire Builder. Up on the street the exodus of office workers from the towers is breathtaking: people spilling onto the sidewalks and over the bridges by the hundreds, by the thousands. I find four postcards and a place that sells stamps.

"Um—how much is postage to Canada?"

The guy looks at me like I'm an idiot. "Now why in the world would I know that?"

I leave without stamps, join the office workers crossing the bridges, follow them this way and that for the next hour. I circle the Grand Opera House, ogle the happy hour patrons at a patio bar by the river. A young woman tugs her three-year-old daughter by the hand, begging passersby for money. The little girl totters on pink shoes. A bride skips by laughing, her bridesmaids scramble to gather up the train of her white dress.

Back in the brown-yellow dinginess of the Amtrak lounge, a platform conductor claps her hands for us to "Get in formation and come through this door here, *single file*. Now y'all get up against the *WALL*! Against the *WALL*, ya hear?"

When we're all through and lined up single file tight to the wall, she leads us a half block down the railroad tracks, back into the building, down a corridor, out another door to where our train waits. The man in front of me is drunk, he pulls his suitcase in a weaving S-curve to the sleeping car. He turns and sticks out his hand,

"Name's Pat! You headin' down for the music?"

Our sleeping car attendant introduces himself as a Basque from Trois-Rivières, Quebec, and shows me to a roomette immediately across the hall from the couple who met, married, and bought a house on three Friday the thirteenths. We stare at each other. The man named Pat clatters by, trying to keep his balance. We're not even moving yet. I can still hear him shouting out his progress to the bar car as the train they call The City of New Orleans rolls out of the station and into the night.

◆　◆　◆

Thursday, May 2. We're somewhere in the Mississippi Delta, just past Yazoo City. I've been drifting for hours with the movement of the train, glimpses of the river through the trees. It's overcast and gray, like home might be—rich green and full-leaved trees, like home would be—then the ratty backsides of little towns as you often see from a train, garbage dumps, and every so often a stand of manicured trees lining a dirt road leading to an old plantation house. I'm clearly far from home.

The guy flying on crack in the room next door—he announced this himself—has begun woohooing with the train whistle, which sounds every ten seconds . . . as it did all night long. Our sleeping car is right behind the engine. Thirteen sleepless hours later, I have no idea why I haven't gone insane. The movement of the train is amazing, more like traveling over the open ocean in a zodiac than rails on ground. I understand now why Miss Dee and Miss Clara in the dining car last night ordered us to hang onto the candy-cane poles between cars and walk with a wide stance. It's not just that half the passengers are drunk. At times the train is rocking so wildly, the double doors between cars line up with each other not straight on but in a perfect "X" shape. And you can see through the accordion pleats to the passing scenery.

We arrived at dawn in Memphis, Tennessee. While the local cops came aboard to look for criminals, I stood on the platform listening to a morning bird song I've never heard before. A very old woman all in purple was taken off the train and picked up, literally, by her sons. They carried her in her wheelchair to a car, appearing so happy and relieved that she'd made the journey intact.

I ate breakfast with Charlie, Joe, and some other guy from Arkansas. They each shook my hand like gentlemen, and Joe began to flirt.

"Take this card here, 'case you're ever in jail in Arkansas. I'm the best lawyer in those parts."

Charlie told me the fields we travelled past were cotton, corn, and wheat, and asked where British Columbia was, "Is it anywhere near Montreal? I was in Montreal once."

I explained that Montreal was at the complete opposite end of the country. Charlie looked disappointed.

The third fellow, who only introduced himself as a lumberman, said he'd heard there was a Quebec somewhere up there near Canada, a "next door" country. I explained that Quebec was a part of Canada, one of the provinces, and that in fact the city of Montreal is in it. The lumberman looked bemused, and doubtful. Clearly not what he'd heard. Charlie raised his hand to ask another question, was it true we were all in Canada still ruled by a *queen*?

Thankfully, at that moment, Miss Clara arrived to save me, "Miss Karin, you finished with your breakfast? Didn't care for your grits?"

"Yes, thank you, Miss Clara, and no, not particularly."

She smiled at me so kindly, whipped the almost untouched bowl of grits away.

So I've spent the last morning of this journey in my little room, drifting with the scenery passing by outside the window, listening to the woohooing of the train whistle and the guy flying on crack in the room next door, my notebook and pen in hand, camera at the ready.

As we slow to a stop in Hazlehurst, Mississippi, my window lines up with a beautiful gray-blue wall opposite, a tiny window in the wall perfectly and asymmetrically placed. I photograph it. I don't know it yet, but it's the first of many photographs of walls and windows to come.

"Conduct the police to the observation car please, the police to the observation car."

It's Miss Dee's voice over the intercom from the dining car—which answers my question of whether to rouse myself from staring at the Mississippi to check out the observation car. I opt for a shower instead, change into "Nola" clothes. I'm not even in New Orleans yet but "Nola" already lives in my vocabulary with ease.

The guy still flying on crack in the room next door begins to sing, then shout. He's realized he left his wallet on the dashboard of his car in Chicago. I poke my head into the hallway, catch eyes with his big blonde girlfriend who's also peeking out, clearly not on drugs herself but clearly needs some.

As we cross into Louisiana, a last lunch with the couple who met, married, and bought a house on three Friday the thirteenths. I've learned things from them the past four days that assure me we live worlds apart, but the three of us will likely remember a few same precious things: Stan and his third-last trip, "steaks medium, potatoes well done," the blizzard in Montana, the woman beginning her new life after her husband left, making it past the floods, spring tulips and rush hour in Chicago, the incessant wail of the train whistle as we bounced down the rails through the Mississippi Delta.

Final approach to Nola, we cross the long bridge over Lake Pontchartrain. I gather my belongings as the train they call The City of New Orleans rolls to a stop. As we disembark, the moisture-laden air hits us first, then the jazz music blaring from speakers on the platform. We stick together through the station, me and the couple who met, married, and bought a house on three Friday the thirteenths. Then they vanish into the taxi line-up. I search the crowds for a driver from the film production, someone holding up a sign with my name on it. There's a sudden flash of light, followed immediately by an unholy clap of thunder. The clouds hanging low overhead let loose.

Three

Landing

I HAVE THREE DAYS TO myself before filming begins. My hotel is in the Warehouse District, and the moment I step out of it, I wish I'd brought my camera today . . . the buildings in states of decay or reconstruction, worn beauty everywhere. I keep seeing the same banner on every second street post: "Welcome to Your Blank Canvas."

At a deli in what I'll come to know as the CBD—Central Business District—I eat half a pastrami sandwich the size of a loaf of bread, then find my way back to the hotel to put the other half in the fridge for dinner. The hotel is really less a hotel than a long-term residence for everyone from folks like me and my colleagues in the film production to construction workers, people working the oil rigs, you name it. The three-story structure surrounds a central patio where it appears that everyone gathers for morning coffee or the evening happy hour. The jazz music stopped piping into the patio at ten p.m. last night, began again at nine this morning. I don't know it yet, but this will be every day for the rest of my stay here. The floor-to-ceiling curving windows of the living room area of my suite on the second floor look out on to the patio, and around to everyone else's rooms on all three other sides of the compound. Great for seeing, and being seen, if that's what you're into. When I arrived last night and stood at the window, looking out I felt much like I was standing on a stage with an audience below, across, and all around me. I closed the drapes. I suspect they'll stay closed.

Where I would dearly have loved to find a window is in the bedroom. But in the bedroom: no windows. Just four brick walls, painted white. With the drapes closed on the windows of my living room stage and four windowless white walls in the bedroom, unless I turn a light on in the suite, it's dark as a cave. Not quite what I was hoping for.

My bedroom backs on to a nothing street, as in there's nothing of interest on it, just a parking lot across the way and the ever-changing sky overhead. Which I must say would be very nice to see from a window. Constance Street, I learned this morning, is its name. I learned this because when I went down to find coffee, as I haven't gone to a grocery store yet, the people I'd met at happy hour last night were all back on the patio and full of morning cheer, wishing me to join them. I'm going to be here for almost four months. A daily coffee klatch is not something I'll be able to sustain in orangutan solitude. So, I waved cheerily and slipped out a side door of the compound, wishing to be outside with my coffee and take in the morning air, but alone. The nothingness of Constance Street behind the hotel, with its gravel parking lot opposite and the sky overhead, this will have to do for my alone space outside.

As I start out again after putting the other half of my monster sandwich in the fridge, I'm wearing every item of warm clothing I brought. It's cold and windy, threatening to pour rain. Last night at the hotel, the people returning from Jazz Fest (soaked through and caked with mud) left their ruined sandals outside their rooms, and at the happy hour on the patio in a break between storms, someone told me there isn't a pair of rubber boots left in the city. So far, it's the coldest, wettest Jazz Fest on record.

I head off in no particular direction, hoping I'm heading for the French Quarter but not knowing for sure, and for some reason not wishing to consult a map. The sun breaks through the clouds, and it starts to warm up, fast. Down Magazine Street to Poydras, across to St. Charles, across Canal to Royal—I look around and grin, knowing instantly I'm there: a man with a washboard and another with a white trombone make music in the middle of the street. Further down there's an a cappella group, then three guys with banjos, then a kid drumming an overturned bucket. People crowd the shops, the restaurants, the sidewalks, Mardi Gras beads hang from three-hundred-year-old balconies. I wander slowly for hours, taking it all in.

Around four o'clock by the old courthouse, waiters spill out of the restaurants untying their aprons, grabbing a smoke between shifts. A while later, I'm outside a small gallery of collage work, art pieces crafted from shoes and bullets and kitchen things. There's a blues duo playing in there, a drummer and a guy on a cigar box guitar. The music is finally too infectious, I find myself dancing a little in the street.

The gallery owner sees me outside, and waves. "Come on in, have a beer!" he calls. "You can join the party or just take it to go!"

I hesitate for the briefest of moments. Then—why not? I go in, join the party.

❖ ❖ ❖

The next morning it's pouring rain again. On the shuttle bus to Jazz Fest, the woman across the aisle from me is very pleased with herself: in the absence of a single pair of rubber boots left for sale in the city, she's had a thinking-outside-the-box moment and wants everyone to know.

"I said, Bob! what about kitchen garbage bags? Couldn't we tie those over our feet? So we popped into the drugstore and grabbed some, I've been giving them to everyone!"

"Don't give no more away," says Bob. "We'll run out."

"Oh you!" She whacks his knee. "We've got lots."

I fish out my wallet and offer her two dollars. "Can I buy some?"

Bob scowls at me. "Yer either from the North Pole or the South. I dunno which."

The rain stops by the time we reach the festival grounds, steam rises from wet hay blanketing the mud. There's a distinct barnyard odor. I buy a program, consult the festival map. Where to begin? I follow the crowds from stage to stage, then see a banner: "Gospel Tent."

It's like hopping on board a musical rocket ship. Neither Christian nor religious, within moments I'm dancing and waving my arms over my head. There's a woman signing lyrics in ASL for the crowd, her body pulsing with the rhythm of the music as her hands do a ballet of language. I decide I want to be an ASL signer for a gospel group when I grow up. An hour later, there's a sudden wedding onstage: a bride, a groom, and however many hundreds of us witnesses yelling "Aaaa - MEN!!"

Then the rocket ship takes off again and sometime during the twentieth chorus of a song whose title must be "My God is Awesome," I start to feel dizzy. It's time to step out of the whirlwind and back into the now-blazing sun. I find barbecue shrimp and a beer, then line up at the port-a-potty. A hatless woman in front of me keels over, stands up, keels over again. People urge her to go to the medic tent. She buries her face in her boyfriend's chest, who explains to everyone that she's embarrassed and just wants to pee.

In the "People's Health and Economy Tent" it's Dixieland jazz and brass bands. During the first chorus of "Bill Bailey Won't You Please Come Home," to my astonishment, an impromptu parade breaks out. People get up and follow each other around the tent in a step-touch to the music. Some with parasols, lace or glittered or tasseled, some with regular umbrellas, some waving colorful hankies, some waving a Kleenex out of their pocket, one man bouncing a skull on a stick. Young and old, fat and thin, black and white and olive-skinned and tan and pale and freckled, one man jaunting along in a wheelchair, an ancient curved-over woman on a cane, a child who just learned to walk and totters along sometimes clapping, sometimes sucking his thumb.

A memory from a year ago suddenly pops into my mind . . . step-touching on the banks of the Yukon River in Whitehorse, Yukon. Six First Nations tribes in a drumming circle led the community in dance. A young girl step-touched up beside me. Purple hair, purple clothes, purple shoes. She held out her hand to me,

"Name Karen."

"Me too," I said.

So I get up and join in now as I did then. And later, as a woman keels over and dies at the Fleetwood Mac concert on the main stage, I'm still step-touching in Dixieland, following what I'll come to know as the second line parade. And still later, waiting with several hundred other people for the shuttle buses back to downtown, the couple in front of me turns and tells me, unprompted, that they're from Baltimore.

"That's where I was born," I say.

"Where did you live?" they ask.

Well, I think, Baltimore's a big city, and I have no clue what suburb or neighborhood we lived in. But I've always remembered the name of the tiny cul-de-sac where our house stood, with five other houses ringing the half circle. Memories of catching fireflies in the dark and popping tar bubbles in the pavement and my little friend Kathy with her wagon of stuffed animals next door, and so many other heart-filled and heart-aching things from early childhood there will never leave me. I've never been back to this house since we left it, but it has stayed vibrant in my memory since. These people from Baltimore certainly wouldn't know this tiny corner of the city, but I tell them anyway,

"We lived at Stoneleigh Court."

"That's where we live," says the woman of the couple, smiling at me as if it was the most unsurprising thing in the world to hear. Her husband bends to buy a beer for himself and Pepsis for his wife and me, from a ten-year-old boy selling them out of a cooler through the wire fence.

❖   ❖   ❖

I have one more day to land myself in New Orleans before work begins. It's time to meet an orangutan. The bus to the zoo stops a block from my hotel, in front of a bar advertising "Free Music and Boiled Crawfish" on Fridays and Sundays. I catch the #11 Uptown to the Garden District, it winds its way along narrow Magazine Street, a few miles to Audubon Park. I'm going to meet Berani, a mature male orangutan, one of three orangutans who live here. For the first time in my life, I have the chance to live in the same city with an orangutan. I hope we can be friends.

I find Berani outside, resting in a hammock. He glances at me, turns away. I find a bench, settle in for the wait. To get to know an orangutan takes patience. Half an hour later, he glances over again. Fifteen minutes later, again. Fifteen minutes later, he swings to a pole and climbs it to stare down at me. I take off my sun hat, offer him a bow, show him how the hat turns inside out and is a different color on the inside. I introduce myself in words, tell him how pleased I am to meet him. He stares. Five minutes later, he climbs down and goes back to his hammock. I wait two more hours. Berani doesn't look at me again.

On the bus back down Magazine eight people hop aboard brandishing cocktails. They're from Alabama, they say, "and we're *drunk*!"

Back at the hotel in my windowless white room, I turn on Nola TV, a station that's all-things Nola. On Nola TV it's also the cocktail hour: a bartender chills a glass, sprays it with lavender, shakes up rye whiskey with bitters and simple syrup, finishes it with a twist of lemon and calls it a Sazerac. You can watch Nola TV 24/7, see a chef setting oysters on fire or someone downing something called Swamp Water or a happy couple sucking crawfish heads or a host of other things. My favorite part of the evening programming is when the lawyer appears. As pictures flash by of people dancing in the streets, he tells us that "bad things do happen to good people" and that when we get tossed in jail, they're gonna take our wallet, our cellphone, and every friend we have in the world. He advises us to write his phone number on a piece of paper and keep it close to us, "as close as you can." The lawyer shows up on Nola TV several times a night.

The next morning on the news the traffic report is about two road closures due to three murders overnight. The closures are a few blocks from my hotel. I make coffee, take it down to enjoy on the patio under the trees, where birds are chirping the dawn and no one else is up yet. I go back upstairs to shower and get ready for work.

Four

Mid May

TEN DAYS INTO MY time here, a feeling prevails: I've landed on another planet. The blazing heat that will only get hotter, the rain when it pours turning the drainpipes on buildings into great hoses blasting the sidewalks and the cars in the street. The jazz music piped into our hotel patio from just below my window from morning until night. The birdsong at dawn in the lilac trees, the absolute still and quiet of night at this end of the Warehouse District, the mayhem of Canal Street and the Quarter a few blocks away. My windowless bedroom, something I thought I'd hate. Instead, it's become a sanctuary, a big cool white room with a fan whirring overhead. At our apartment at home in Vancouver, I wake to every West End noise . . . here in the first week alone I slept through three storms. Wi-Fi at the hotel is sporadic at best. Home feels further and further away.

After long, hot, grueling days at work, I come back to the white room, craving . . . something. One night I walk to the restaurant that advertises free music and crawfish on Fridays and Sundays. It's later on a weekday evening, so I'm the last customer and alone. I sit sweating on their patio in the dark with a plate of fried pickles and a cool drink. Another evening I stroll with the crowds down Magazine to Canal Street and the souvenir and liquor shops, back up Fulton and Tchoupitoulas past the restaurants and bars. I step through white flower petals strewn the length of a block, a man walking four beagles on individual leashes ahead of me. Another evening I walk a circle of blocks near the hotel and pass three art gallery openings. Inside, people sip wine and chat in front of the paintings. I already know enough of this city to know I'm welcome to join them, but I don't.

One evening I take a glass of wine down to the patio to enjoy under the trees. There's no bugs or mosquitoes yet, but I understand they're coming by the hordes with the summer heat. How it will get hotter is hard to imagine, but I'm told it will. Everyone has gone to bed, the hotel is silent. I'm wide awake. I go back up to my room, find the pair of smaller arm hula hoops a friend made for me to bring on the trip. Because they're small they're fast and difficult, harder to maneuver than large hoops. I find a space on the soft mat of the tennis court where I can drop them as often as I know I'm going to, and begin. A man who I don't know yet as Edgar the security guard comes out of the office, watches for a moment, then carries on with his rounds.

The whimsy of the hotel Wi-Fi connection is driving me nuts. As the next storm rolls in and the tv news announces we're under a flash flood warning, I decide to take internet connectivity into my own hands. I put on my new yellow rain poncho (Walgreens, eight bucks) and head out. The St. Charles Streetcar is packed with other poncho-clad passengers, all of us pouring sweat under our plastic. It's raining sideways in on us through the open windows, a blessed bit of cool as we ca-lunk ca-lunk round Lee Circle and up St. Charles Avenue. By the time I reach the AT&T store, I'm a walking puddle.

A nice young man named Kendall tries in various ways to encourage my iPad to accept an AT&T chip card and for various reasons, no luck. I leave sodden and dejected, stop and think about it, go back in.

Half an hour later, I'm the proud owner of a brand-new iPad mini in an eye-catching hot pink case. My new best friend Kendall puts in an AT&T chip and fires up internet connectivity on it. I'm good to go.

The next day is Mother's Day. I've heard there's going to be a second line parade near the Quarter, on Frenchmen Street. I think about wandering down to check it out, but it's raining again and we're still under a flash flood warning, so I dawdle around my white room making a list of things I'll need over the next few months: can opener, placemat, thermos, good knife, Q-tips, toothbrushes, witch hazel, hand weights, frying pan, yoga mat, extra socks, padded envelopes, Scotch tape, salad spinner, veggie wash, Band-aids, dish mat, batteries, beach towel, umbrella(!), juice jug, laundry detergent, spritzer bottles. I've discovered that the shopping possibilities in the Warehouse District are slim. There's one fabulous grocery store, six long blocks away, Rouses, where you can scoop fresh-boiled crawfish from a cooler at eleven a.m. precisely every morning, and find the best of every imaginable ingredient for the best of every imaginable gourmet dish. There's a Walgreens seven longer blocks away on Canal Street, another direction. Then the liquor and souvenir shops. But that's pretty much it. I need to go to the one store in miles that has *everything* . . . Walmart.

The cabbie drives under the freeway into a derelict neighborhood by the river, past warehouses and a condemned power plant, into a parking lot the size of a football field and crammed to bursting. I can't believe I'm actually doing this, and I'm almost ashamed to admit it: I'm excited. I grab a shopping cart big enough to hold six kids, line up for a burger and coke at McDonald's, get out my list, and begin stalking the aisles. How it happens I don't know, but somehow my cart fills not just with the items on my list but a host of other things I suddenly and absolutely must have: a yellow tank top, a twelve-pack of peanut butter cups, a box of root touch-up, a turquoise head band, a jar of peanuts, a big bottle of mouthwash, a package of razors, a bottle of hydrogen peroxide, a gallon of water, seven feet of bubble wrap, four Starbucks vanilla Frappuccinos, a package of make-up remover pads, two tins of smoked mussels, a mascara, three cans of tuna, two cans of mushroom soup, a tin of salmon, two glow-in-the-dark hula hoops (one pink, one yellow), an eight-pack of Pepsi minis, and a snack bag of potato chips.

I turn on my phone to see what time it is. Four o'clock. I've been here over two hours. I check the messages. There's just one, from home: "Please let us know you're okay ASAP."

What on earth? Did the flash flood hit and make the news back in Canada? I ask people around me, no one seems to know or care. Like me, they're lost in a shopping daze. I message back, "I'm fine! Just shopping at Walmart!"

When I get back to the windowless white room with my ten bags of purchases, I turn on the tv news and stop cold. At the Mother's Day second line parade this afternoon, a man pulled out a gun and began shooting. Nineteen people were hit, some now in critical condition, some of them children. Like the second line I leapt to join at Jazz Fest, if I'd been there today, I would have joined this one too.

◆　◆　◆

The next day, I head back to the Quarter. When I first went, I'd begun in the middle, with Royal Street. Today, I start at the edge. Twelve blocks of Decatur Street, nothing delights me. Round the corner to the French Market, the crush of tourists is overwhelming. Tables and tables of cheap sunglasses, hats, sundresses, souvenirs. I cross the railroad tracks, up to a path along the Mississippi. Brown water. Industrial area beyond. A woman whooping from the deck of a paddle wheeler on her eighty-nine-dollar lunch cruise. I hate cheap souvenirs and lunch cruises.

I wonder exactly where I am. I still haven't looked at a map, don't know why. A month from now when I finally do, I'll find Frenchmen Street on it. I'll wonder how it was possible, the day after such violence and near tragedy so few blocks from where I stand, there could be no trace of it on these streets. People still packing into Café Du Monde to tear into their beignets, tap their fingers to the beat of a jazz combo.

Before I came here, I was given three rules for a successful visit by people who knew New Orleans. One, don't go in summer. Two, stay a week or two at most. Three, if you're a woman alone, don't venture off the tourist path. I look left to the brown Mississippi, right to the crowds of tourists in the Quarter. A tightness creeps into my chest, not helped by the suffocating moist heat. I've broken the first two rules for a successful visit. I don't yet know how, but I'm going to have to start breaking the third.

A few days later, I make my way back to the orangutans. Berani stares past me as if I don't exist. I realize: there's no special friendship coming. I watch a small lizard exploring the base of a tree. He looks up, puffs out his throat sac. There's a tingle at the back of my neck, the sense of something behind me . . .

A gorilla. In the enclosure across from the orangutans. Sitting on a stone shelf, staring at me through the fence. I get up, walk one way past the people watching him, then all the way back the other. His eyes follow me. I get out my iPhone, Google "name of silverback gorilla at Audubon Zoo."

Casey.

When the crowds leave, I approach the fence.

"Name Karin," I say, my hand to my chest. I take off my hat, offer him a bow. "You Casey. Nice to meet you." I speak and sign to him in the same made-up pidgin sign language I use with my orangutan friends back in Seattle.

Casey looks away. Back to me. He sniffs the air, deeply. He settles himself on the stone shelf, his eyes holding mine.

❖   ❖   ❖

Back at the hotel, it's dusk before eight o'clock, darkness soon after. At ten, the jazz music piped into the hotel patio since nine this morning shuts off, and most people go to bed. As I've begun doing almost every night, I grab my arm hoops and a bottle of water and head down. The soft mat of the tennis court is still hot to the touch, the air roasting. I haven't twirled a hoop yet, already pouring sweat.

I began hooping last September. I'm still wondering what exactly it is about it that holds my attention. Besides the exercise and fun of it, the fun of finding a circus trick, the relaxed and meditative focus it asks while still allowing me to *do* something. I practice arm circles to the side, overhead and under, hand changes, tosses, rolls over the backs of my hands. Dropping the hoops over and over again, it seems impossible to sustain a flow. Edgar the security guard comes out, watches for a moment, carries on with his rounds. I keep practicing and dropping hoops, remind myself that nobody cares if I'm good at it or not. Really, it doesn't matter, it has no obvious worth in my life. The thought stops me for a second. Then I continue practicing, dropping hoops. Perhaps the lack of importance is why I love it most. At midnight, I retreat to the windowless white room and an ice-cold shower. Somehow more myself.

I go back to see Casey the next day. He notes me immediately, his eyes follow as I go to sit on the bench in the shade of the tree. A family joins me on the bench, their curly-haired toddler climbs onto my back and clasps her hands round my neck.

"Rae-Rae!" gasps her mother. "Come to your mama, leave the lady alone!"

"I don't mind," I say.

Rae-Rae plays with my shirt collar, Casey watches. Suddenly there's an unholy noise and three F-16 fighter jets pass by overhead. The gorillas go nuts, racing round the enclosure.

I decide to walk the whole way back to the Warehouse District, along Magazine Street. It's a few miles. Along the way I find Café Luna in a tumbling-down mansion at the corner of Nashville and Magazine. Dog-eared books over the fireplace—everything from medical texts to romance novels—and as I'll soon learn, a pony-tailed barista who doesn't mind if you sit for hours on his sloping porch sipping a coffee, watching lizards dart between the tables. You can feel it right away: a place to breathe, think, write.

The next day I bring my hoops along, take the St. Charles Streetcar up to the other side of Audubon Park, walk the mile through it to the zoo. It hits me how much I miss the smell of green. At home I live near a large park, and while the Warehouse District is rich in bricks and history, there's not much green. I stop beside the bayou to practice higher and higher tosses and catches with my hoops under the trees. A turtle watches me from a rock, then something with a flat head peeks out of the water, circles briefly, disappears again.

Casey is at the ready when I arrive. As I sit on the shaded bench, he moves immediately to his stone shelf seat with its rock shade overhang, and gazes steadily at me, sniffing the air. I've had the chance to get to know a few gorillas, but I've never known one to stare at me like this. Much less be okay with me staring right back. It's blazing hot this afternoon. No other visitors at the moment, and all the other gorillas off sleeping somewhere. Same with the orangutans in the enclosure behind me. Casey and I sit together in some kind of shared solitude, holding each other's eyes. I wonder where this is heading?

After visiting with Casey, I'm about to hop on the #11 bus back down Magazine when I see a bus heading the opposite direction, who knows where. I cross the street and get on it. After ten minutes or so it turns past a village center, there's a crowd lined up under a big sign: "Thirtieth Anniversary Sale, Two for One."

I get off the bus and join the crowd. "What are we lining up for?"

Three large women in big hats turn to stare at me. "Daiquiris, hon'. What else? Two-for-one take-out, any size."

When we get to the front of the line, the three ladies order quart-size, two each. I look at the rainbow of alcoholic flavors swirling in chillers on the wall, ask for a small of whatever is the least sweet, and just one please. I'm given two. The big ladies swilling their quarts two-fisted are happy to take the other one off my hands and ask, do I know that the Dalai Lama is in town?

I don't know this. But as I hop back on a bus, carrying a cocktail onto it for the first time in my life and feeling quite merry, it starts to seem like a good idea to find him.

❖　❖　❖

To my astonishment, I find the Dalai Lama a mere block from my hotel. But the security guard who stands in front of me with crossed arms says I'm too late, the event is sold out and almost over. Dejected, I wander back down to the main floor of the Convention Center. There's a group of people clustered around a roped-off area, others sit about meditating. I don't want to meditate. I want to see the Dalai Lama. Or at least one of the Tibetan monks I've learned are here with him. Supposedly they've been crafting a mandala out of individual grains of colored sand for the past three days. Where the hell is it?

A space opens up by the roped-off area. I step into it and gasp. There it is. The sand mandala. It's exquisite. Three feet across and more intricate than I could possibly have imagined. We all stand silent, staring at it. An hour later, the Tibetan monks arrive. They perform a chant over the mandala, the sound is unearthly. Then it comes time for them to destroy their work, sweep the sand mandala into little bags. I didn't know this was coming and the seemingly effortless destruction of their creation knocks me back, like a hit to the chest. I close my eyes. Can't watch.

More and more people have gathered. By the time the Tibetan monks are leaving with their bags of sand, a thousand or so of us follow them into the street. Where are we going, and why? I have no clue but don't want to ask. A heavy police presence surrounds us, perhaps the tragedy of the Mother's Day second line parade still fresh in mind. Our procession makes its way to Mardi Gras World, through the warehouse where the floats are stored. It's more than a little strange, following the bobbing orange headdresses of the monks past ten-foot-tall princesses and tuxedo-clad bunnies, superheroes and gold statues of Buddha, and all manner of other frozen-faced things. The monks' chant echoes through the space. We make our way to the Mississippi River, where the thousand or so of us stand witness as the monks scatter the remains of their sand mandala into the brown water rolling by, to send healing energy into the world. I make my way slowly back to my windowless white room, and eat a sandwich.

The next morning, I find the weekly farmers' market in a parking lot two blocks away, come back with baby cucumbers and zucchini, red turnips and big yellow tomatoes. In the afternoon, I hop the St. Charles Streetcar up to a grand old mansion once the home of a silent-screen star, now a library. I get a library card and take out two books on Hurricane Katrina. I've got a plan to begin reading the history of this city, moving backwards.

That night after dark, as usual, I'm out with my hoops on the tennis court. Then: like the click that happens when you can suddenly ride a bike, the smallest hoops begin to twirl in my hands. Fast and slow, high and low, two at once, going the same way or in opposite directions. I watch in amazement as they keep going and going. A flash of light in the night sky above me catches my eye and finally, the hoops drop. What is it? Looks like a tiny fire just above the roof of the hotel. It flies past. Then another, and another, and another, and another. Some tiny fires turning somersaults, some low overhead, some further away, coming by the dozens now in a haphazard procession against the night sky. What on earth? At last, I see what they are: they're paper bags holding lit candles. There's people still out on the patio with their cocktails, no one else glances up. Edgar the security guard comes out of the office. I smile at him and am about to point up when he nods and smiles and points up: yes, I see them too.

Sunday morning in the Warehouse District, hot and still. As the bells ring for mass at the cathedral round the corner, I get out my camera for the first time since I arrived and step into my neighborhood. I find myself focusing on smaller and smaller pieces of buildings until I get the ah hah! that says, yes, this is it, this is the photograph. A grouping of bricks. Numbers beside a doorway. Paint peeling from a drainpipe. A crack in the sidewalk. A windowsill. Once the pictures begin to arrive, they don't stop.

Five

Late May

AT WORK, THE CIRCUMSTANCES we find ourselves in become more and more challenging. One of the locations is so grim, I come back to the windowless white room each night wheezing and stinking to high heaven of something namelessly awful. I stand in the shower until I can breathe better, but the stink never quite leaves, and I've noticed some sort of rash starting on one leg, a weird-looking infection on the other foot. Thank goodness for the hydrogen peroxide I got at Walmart, I'm liberal with it. In late May, a brief hiatus is called. I decide to hop a bus to Atlanta.

I have friends who work at the zoo there, who will introduce me to Chantek. Chantek is one of the only orangutans in the world who learned sign language when he was part of language research studies when he was young. Now, thankfully in sanctuary at Zoo Atlanta with a family of fellow orangutans, he no longer needs to sign. But, playing an orangutan character who communicates through sign language, I'm excited to meet him.

It's nice to get out of town for a few days, even on a bus. At the Greyhound station in Mobile, Alabama, a man chases pigeons around the parking lot, explaining to them how Peter is the man to follow, not

Jesus. Another man in a lime-yellow vest sweeps cigarette butts, two others sit smoking and comparing notes about Bourbon Street. One was shot and lifts his bandage to show off the wound, the other tells of passing out over his drink and waking up under a mattress. Both are "damn glad" to be out of New Orleans, they say.

Inside the station, waiting passengers watch a blonde woman on tv discuss "male congenital childhood syndrome." There's a wall of video games, one with a life-size rifle you can hold. You make points by bagging a bunny or a deer or any number of other woodland creatures. I order a burger from a woman with gold teeth who won't let me tip her, it's not allowed, she says. The burger is delicious.

Back on the bus I close myself off to all but the Scotch pines and hills rolling by outside the window. In the ninth hour of our twelve-hour trip, a man hollers his way up the aisle to the driver, he forgot to get off in Montgomery to go to Birmingham. The bus weaves on the highway as our driver explains to the man, with gestures, the error of his thinking,

"If y'all think we turnin' around *now* when y'all can't read your own *ticket*?"

When we get off in Atlanta, it's dark and panhandlers descend. At a convenience store by the taxi stand, I ask the clerk behind his bullet-proof glass if he sells water and red wine. He comes out and opens a refrigerator, points to Wild Rose Whisky.

"That's what we got."

I leave with a big bottle of water. At the hotel in New Orleans the water out of the tap is undrinkable, so once a week I walk the six blocks to Rouses and lug a couple four-gallon jugs back. I don't know what the water will be like at the hotel in Atlanta, but I don't want to be thirsty.

In the cab my driver turns to look at me grimly and says, "You are my bad news."

He goes on to explain how he's waited and prayed for fourteen hours for a "big money ride," and I am not that. He continues to moan "bad news, bad news" until I ask him to please stop doing that. He drives the rest of the way in silence, but watching him in the rearview mirror, I can still see his lips moving.

❖   ❖   ❖

The hotel seems lovely, a step up from our compound in Nola. There's Wi-Fi and bottled water and a restaurant and bar, and in the morning a free hotel shuttle, the driver happy to drive me to the zoo and come back to get me, just call him when I'm ready, he says. How nice.

I meet up with my friends, and ten minutes after we arrive at the orangutan habitat I'm crouched beside a mesh fence, watching an orangutan mother make a decision. Blaze holds her baby Pongo to her chin and studies my eyes above the surgical mask. She looks to the people on either side of me, that she knows and trusts. She decides: yes, the stranger is safe. Holding baby Pongo right in front of me she helps him eat—wiping cereal from his lips, waking him when he nods off. Her welcome takes my breath. Pongo's father Benny twirls slowly like a dancer down his hallway and back again, peeking at me. Who's the stranger come to visit? Further down, surrogate mother Madu has her hands full with two teenaged boys who are literally falling over each other to show off, look what I can do with torn paper! No, watch *me*. No, watch ME!

Then there's Alan. A mature male who bears an uncanny resemblance to the only orangutan I've come to know from the inside out, the one I live and breathe each day at work but who doesn't tangibly exist. Alan is almost a dead ringer for what my orangutan character looks like. Beyond that, there's something extraordinary about Alan and the moment we catch eyes, I'm a goner. Behind him, his female companion

Biji hangs back, her brow furrowed, studying me suspiciously.

Moving outside, we meet Nicky. She steps to the edge of a moat, her eyes shy—who are you? Then there's Chantek. He hangs above us in a hammock, won't come to stay hello. My friends go back to work and I'm allowed to stay there, me on one side of the moat, Nicky and Chantek on the other. For the first time in my life, I'm alone with orangutans. Nicky looks at me, what you got?

I got nothing. No paints, no crayons, nothing. Chantek continues to study me through the mesh of his hammock. I sign to him, in carefully practiced ASL, "Nice to meet you, can we be friends?" No answer, not a twitch.

I remember the travel sketchbook I carry with me and lo and behold, I find a tiny box of watercolors with it. As I do with my orangutan friends in Seattle, I turn the paper facing away from myself towards Nicky and begin to paint. Strips of color, blocks of color, flowers. Nicky creeps closer. From my perspective peeking over the edge of the paper, I start an upside-down tree. There's a shadow beside Nicky. Chantek has joined us. I dab red blotches on the green of the tree, an orange sun beside it. Chantek lifts a lazy fist to his cheek, taps his wrists together. I ask a keeper friend who's just arrived with snack treats what he said.

"Apple. Work," she says. She explains that "work" is what he calls painting. Jaw agape, I look from the red paint daubs of apples on my tree to Chantek, who observes me steadily.

The conversation in painting with Nicky and Chantek, and Alan and Biji, continues for three days. Alan and I fall in something with each other. I learn that he loves sparkly rings and wonder, how to give him a ring of his own? Biji continues to hide behind him, watching the painting with a furrowed brow. Each time I leave though, she swings from the shadows to follow me to the very edge of her enclosure.

Chantek and Nicky settle at the edge of the moat, their eyes on my paper, ready. In the silence between their watching and my hand moving color over paper, the fullness of their presence is astounding. I grow uncomfortable with the quiet, start to chatter at Chantek, aloud and with my hands. He stares back at me, not answering. The smell of silverback gorillas in a habitat just over the hill drifts past. They can't see me, but I think they know I'm here.

At night, back at the hotel, I stare out the window, twelve floors down to the restaurant patio, out to the city beyond. After a day reflected back to me in orangutan eyes, civilization looks so strange. I try to remember what I've learned about who. Is it Chantek who likes to do beading? Biji who likes to weave? Alan who likes coloring books? Who is it that makes brooms and organizes things?

The next day, after lunch at the café across the street from the zoo, I ask if they have any cardboard toilet paper roll inserts in the garbage. They don't, but (looking at me strangely) sell me a full roll for a dollar. I've had a silly brain wave, and at the end of the day before going out to dinner with my human friends, set myself up on a picnic bench in the park, take all the toilet paper off the roll, and start to paint the cardboard insert. I found a drugstore last night where I bought non-toxic kids' paint. If Alan is to have a ring of his own it must be something he can eat.

The next morning I'm chattering at Chantek again as I paint, aloud and with my hands. I've given up hoping for an answer but taught myself some new sign language anyways,

"I like to paint. It's nice. Would *you* like to paint?"

Suddenly Chantek lifts his head, sighs, and makes a face. He does a sharp, annoyed palms-up gesture that makes me laugh. I don't need a translator to understand his response,

"With what."

In the keeper office I find a knife and saw the painted toilet paper insert into five ragged rings. My keeper friends and I bring them to Alan. He takes one on his finger, flings it off like it bit him. A second try, he bats the ring further away and stares at it. Meantime Biji has received one too, she's considering it. A third try with Alan, this time he keeps the ring on long enough for me to get a few pictures before gently waving his finger for it to be removed. He looks at the ring on the floor of the enclosure, back to me.

Nicky and Chantek are watching for us. They follow as we climb the hill to where the rings can be tossed down to them. Nicky tears hers apart and eats it. Chantek stares at his on the ground: No. Flipping. Way.

Then: Nicky looks at Chantek's ring. She goes over and bats at it, picks it up, thinks. Ever so carefully, she puts it over two of her toes. She takes off in a little happy dance around the yard. As enrichment for orangutans goes, aside from Nicky's reaction I know it's pretty much a bust. As enrichment for visiting strangers, priceless.

Back at the hotel, I can't bear to go up to my room yet. I'm leaving in the morning and so sad to go. I can't believe how deeply these new orangutan friends have reached me in three short days. It's not quite sunset, there's a gentle breeze. The restaurant patio and driveway in front of the hotel is jolly with guests heading out on this Saturday evening. The hotel is packed, many ladies heading out in full ball gowns with big hair-dos and high heels. A bit surprising for what I've heard is a church convention. I find a quiet chair on the patio and back myself to the wall nearest the door leading inside to the restaurant, cuddle my purse on my lap with the strap over my head and around my body, as I'm careful to do anywhere I might stop in New Orleans. In broad daylight on a restaurant patio like this at such a nice hotel, where everyone has been so kind and I'm in the middle of a church convention, probably not necessary to be so cautious, but I am anyway. I get out my beloved new iPad mini in its hot pink case and with delight, scroll through pictures of the ring on Alan's finger. The iPad rings with a Skype call from my partner Tom back in Vancouver. I launch into telling him everything about these magical three days.

Then it happens, and so fast. Out of nowhere two men jump on top of me. One pins me down hard while the other grabs the iPad from my hands and tries to rip my purse from around my body. I hold onto the purse for dear life. It probably lasts less than twenty seconds, the guy pinning me down lets go, and the two of them run to the edge of the restaurant patio with my iPad mini, leap the fence and into a waiting car that takes off fast towards the freeway. I'm on my feet screaming, the ladies in ball gowns turn to stare. Two more men run out of the bar, take off in fruitless pursuit of the thieves.

A woman comes up to me, "Are you okay?"

I'm not and keep screaming. I run for the hotel business center and, still screaming and shaking, get into a computer and change every password, every trace to my identity, as fast as I can. The hotel clerks do . . . nothing. An hour later, a police woman shows up bored and impatient, gets her report. The restaurant and bar staff and security guards all vow they saw . . . nothing. There's a security camera behind the bar in the restaurant, where the thieves ran out from. The bartender says there would likely be . . . nothing on it.

I go up to my room and sit there and shake. All night long. At four in the morning, I go down to the front desk to ask if it's okay if I pay my bill in cash. I've put a block on my Visa card. The clerk stares at me, takes a bite of her sandwich. When she finishes chewing, she answers, ever so slowly,

"I'm busy. I'm eating my lunch."

Four hours later I'm tucked into a roomette on a train they call The Crescent, heading back to New Orleans. Still shaking. The sensation of having been mugged is new to me. I cuddle into the pillows by the window, watch towns with musical names go by. I try to keep the faces of my new orangutan friends firmly planted in my mind's eye, urge myself to breathe and keep going.

◈   ◆   ◆

Back in Nola and the windowless white room, I find the mugging has brought me to a choice: succumb to fear of everything or . . . not. The choice pops up repeatedly for days. What disturbs me most is the sense that if I'm fearful and still out exploring I'm a sitting duck.

At night after long days at work, I bring my hoops down to the tennis court on the patio. Spinning them under the trees settles me somewhat. Edgar the security guard pauses on his rounds to watch from a respectful distance. We nod to each other, he carries on.

One night on the way back upstairs to my room, a young boy suddenly rushes at me out of the darkness,

"Hullo, my friend," he says.

I've never seen him before in my life. He plants himself in front of me, searches my face for a long moment. Finally, he lets me pass. When I get to my room it occurs to me that I was too surprised to introduce myself, or ask his name.

The next morning while I'm having coffee on the patio, the boy who rushed at me out of the darkness appears again at my elbow,

"For you, my friend." He hands me the tiniest piece of a flower, smiles, and vanishes.

I take it upstairs and put it on my bedside table and stare at it. I realize: I'm ready to explore the world again. Then: for the second time, I forgot to ask his name.

Six

June

AN OLD FRIEND I haven't seen in fifteen years comes to town. We stroll the French Quarter and perch on a restaurant balcony over Royal Street, taking in the setting sun over ancient rooftops and how the passage of time has worn, or not, on each other. The sagging balcony is barely two feet wide and tilting. Without a napkin under my wine glass, it would skid off the table into the crowds on the street below. It's the second time in thirty years my friend and I have seen each other, since we were boyfriend and girlfriend in high school. Every so often, like something on the breeze, I catch a sense of who we each were way back then. It seems we are both, in the essence of ourselves, surprisingly still intact. I wouldn't dare say that out loud, my friend's impression might be different.

My friend leaves town, I keep working. The circumstances we're filming in continue to be challenging, and the hotel patio has begun to feel like the gated compound it is. A bass beat from the incessant jazz music drums into my room and brain even through closed windows. Any day I'm not working I escape, keeping to my inner orangutan solitude but soaking in as much of the city as I can. I've found a way to work with the heat and keep walking: a lunch bag filled with ice pack, frozen towels, and spritzer bottle.

Some days I just wander taking pictures—casement windows, a lady selling knitted baby hats shaped like the tops of vegetables on a street corner, a grumpy cat in a doorway. Other days I choose a particular direction, like to the farmers' market in Louis Armstrong Park. On the way down through the Quarter I stop at Napoleon's Bar, a house built for him in 1797, never lived in. I have my first muffuletta and fresh lemonade there. A classical piano concerto fills the dark room like a cool rain, the first classical music I've heard here. I walk down Chartres to Esplanade, Esplanade to Rampart, turn left. I see three men on different corners of the intersection signal to each other before one approaches me.

"Lady! You got a cellphone I can borrow?"

I walk on, a chill at my back all the way home.

Like puzzle pieces slipping out of a crack in a box, in random order and with no obvious pattern forming yet, New Orleans gains substance for me. I find it on the St. Charles Streetcar, watching a waiter on his way to work nodding to music on his iPod, a freshly-pressed white apron over one knee. I find it in the cockroaches as big as peanuts that have begun to prowl the patio, the tiny green lizards climbing the walls, the whistle-bell tones of cicadas at night. I find it in the drivers on the #11 bus up Magazine who greet me like a local now and chat about stuff. Traffic tie-ups, weather, what they're doing after work. Remember when such and such restaurant was called so and so?

"No, I don't."

"Well, that was fifteen years ago, I have a hard time remembering that far back too."

I find New Orleans in the tumbling-down old mansion that is now "my" library because I have a card, in the book on Hurricane Katrina I'm reading and the images I can't imagine seeing: bodies floating down the street, police holed up in the pharmaceutical department of the very same Walmart I shopped at, sheer hell at the Superdome. I find it at a garage sale on a Saturday morning, in a woman yelling at me across the street on a Wednesday night,

"What you up to this evening? Wanna come judge a poetry competition?"

I find New Orleans in the neighborhood village of Freret at the Bloomin' Deals second-hand store and in the blocks I walked along Napoleon to get there: nice house, nice house, nice house, broken-down house, nice house, overgrown lot, mansion. I find it in the impromptu mayhem of a second line parade party that wasn't there when I got off the streetcar at this corner three hours ago—now there are hundreds of people dancing on the tracks, the streetcar isn't going *anywhere*. I can stand frustrated and wait for them to leave, or dance along with them for another mile when they do. I choose to join them, and dance.

I find New Orleans at PJ's Coffee at Girod and Julia, where I sit outside on Sunday mornings, pouring sweat. The bells at the two-hundred-year-old cathedral up the block ring out, tiny birds hover begging sesame seeds from my bagel. I find it at Carmo's Cafe, where on the hottest of all days, lugging water home from Rouses, a woman makes me a hydrating smoothie from exotic fruits I've never heard of. I find New Orleans in the lugging of water, six blocks in the searing noonday sun, the air thick as butter. I find it in the toothless woman at the Shell station who sells me bottles of juice, in the Italian joint across the street where Stephanie (who's not remotely Italian) remembers my name from one visit, two weeks until the next.

Maybe most happily, I find New Orleans in the pictures I've been taking, often of the smallest things: a crack in the sidewalk, zippers from 1948 still on sale in Clements' Hardware, a man's tie on a drainpipe on Julia Street. I find New Orleans in Casey the gorilla's face.

I find it in my windowless white room which I've learned in 1822 was Saint Mary's Market, the same bricks now painted white. I find it in Edgar the security guard, Leslie and Miss Claudia at the front desk, who always ask to hear about my day and celebrate my finds, Dwayne, who calls me Miss Karin and brings kitchen towels every week when every week the housekeeper forgets. I find New Orleans in the nameless boy who continues to rush at me with pieces of flowers,

"Hullo, my friend! This is for you."

The fifth time this happens, I see the Velcro straps on his shoes flapping as he runs. When I point this out to him,

"It's because they're broken," he says.

I smile at him. "May I?"

He watches intently as I kneel down and do up his shoes. When I sit back up in my chair, he considers me for a moment.

"Do you know Bad Piggies?" he asks.

"No, I don't."

"You need a one-shooter or a two-shooter."

"I see."

He considers me another long moment. "Soon, I will show you how to play."

❖   ❖   ❖

On a sweltering Saturday morning in PJ's Coffee, they're playing Astor Piazzolla tangos. The Argentinian tangos are somehow perfect for the heat. At the farmers' market I take pictures of the pecan lady with her pecans, the Creole tomato lady with her tomatoes. I make my way to the library again, then on the streetcar home, a grown man in a cowboy hat sort of rides a small toy horse. He bought it at a garage sale, he says. He seems quite proud of it. He stays at the front of the streetcar and makes the horse whinny at every passenger who gets on or off. Back at the hotel patio my nameless young friend appears. He stares at a man sitting beside me,

"You're in my seat," he says.

The man gets up and moves. My friend takes his chair and studies me.

"What's your name?" he asks.

"Karin. What's yours?"

"Elijah. Do you know Super Mario?"

"No," I say.

"Okay," he says. "Now we play."

His hands begin to trace the progress of an imaginary computer game in the air between us. He tells me when we've won a game, when we go to the next level. When his father calls to him he races to pick a tiny purple flower and brings it to me. He runs off.

Upstairs I look at my completely unused living room alcove, with its window curtains still drawn shut since the day I arrived. A surprising thought: remove the furniture. Half an hour later of tugging and hefting, I call the front desk. Two strong men and fifteen more minutes later, the couch in its two pieces is stored in a closet down the hall. My yoga mat, weights, hoops and pictures of my Seattle orangutan friends now edge the walls. I step into the empty space. Six weeks into my stay here, I'll begin to occupy it.

There's a birthday party at the zoo for orangutan Menari, she's turning four. After the mayhem of gift opening for both orangutans and gorillas, Casey comes to sit and stare fiercely. Whatever he's giving me I don't fully understand, but I've grown sure that it's one of the things I've come on this journey to get. Back at Café Luna for lunch, I join the regulars on the porch and write like the wind. I walk two miles of Magazine Street before getting on a bus. The sun glints on Mardi Gras beads on a fence.

❖   ❖   ❖

An aging ballet dancer has arrived at the hotel, she's in town to judge a competition, she says. In the evenings, she sits on the patio chain-smoking and drinking straight Scotch, flirting with a group of fellows who call themselves "reconstruction specialists," in town to oversee a building tear-out.

"I'm sixty-five," says the ballet dancer. "Don't look a day over fifty!" She recrosses her legs, her skirt whipping.

"Nice," says the heftiest reconstruction specialist. "I saw 'The Nutcracker' once."

On the tennis court two boys play with a basketball. Elijah jumps on the sidelines, dying to join in. When the ball flies out of reach he sprints to retrieve it for them. They take the ball, don't invite him to play.

The heat is oppressive, we've been under an advisory for a week. Working outside in it is hell, the rest of the time it's like moving in a gentle stupor. I crave things I've never craved before—iced coffees with lots of sugar and cream, meat, potato chips. My days when I'm not working have found a rhythm: morning yoga and weights in the now empty space of my living room alcove, an adventure into the city, late afternoon collapse in the windowless white room. I've grown used to pouring sweat from morning until night, being eaten alive by insects the moment I step out the door. Evenings after everyone goes to bed, I bring my hoops to the tennis court. I've begun exploring and writing down a choreography of sorts, feeling for connections between move-ments, how a particular circling of the hoops can lead to another. I'm not searching for what might look nice but rather feeling it from the inside out: if I'm doing such and such movement with the hoops, what does that prompt me to do next? And then next? I find my way through a sequence of movements for a few minutes, stop, close my eyes, try to begin at the beginning again and remember in my body the hooping sequence, try to sustain it in a brief flow. Often my body forgets completely what I did before and comes up with something else. Once in a while a sequence holds inside me, and I can repeat it. When that happens, I kneel on the still-hot-to-the-touch mat of the tennis court to write it down in my little travel sketchbook, on the pages following the apple tree and other paintings I did for the orangutans in Atlanta. What I'm going to do with these phrases of hoop choreography, I have no idea. Probably nothing.

One evening the boys who play basketball haven't finished their game yet. I wait with my hoops for them to finish so I can take their spot.

"Hullo, my friend!"

It's Elijah at my elbow with a surprise: he's wearing a big black moustache. One corner has come unglued. I help him put it back on. He runs to find me three flowers—pink, white, and red.

My friends back at the zoo in Seattle have introduced me to the orangutan and gorilla keepers at the zoo here. I'm invited for a private introduction to Casey and the other gorillas, and to Berani the orangutan. I arrive an hour early for the meeting, to give Casey a chance to see that I'm there and visit from a distance before meeting me up close. But it's a terribly hot day and when I arrive, he and all the other gorillas are off hiding in the shade somewhere. When it's time for the private introduction, something in me knows better than to go . . . but I do anyway.

The moment Casey sees me he goes nuts. After storming the yard and upsetting the crap out of the other gorillas, he comes to the mesh fence and fixes on me with direct and clearly amorous intent. It's very surprising to the generous person who brought me here, and not her fault. She's not the one who should have known better. Retreat. Regret. How stupidly unfair of me. Casey had no idea that I was coming today, and so close. He had no time to prepare. The meeting with Berani is pleasant and unmagical, all I can think about is how I just embarrassed a good new friend.

Evening on the hotel patio, the ballet dancer is into her Scotch. She's joined a table of couples discussing sexual partner-swapping possibilities. I walk by with my hoops, watch Elijah watching them. When he sees me, he follows to the tennis court, a fresh flower between his fingers. Suddenly he stops, and doesn't approach. He stands and watches as I sweat and spin, spin, spin my regret about Casey into the night.

When I return to see Casey, I immediately bow and apologize. I'm prepared for him to turn his back, storm the yard or just leave. Instead, he watches from a distant wall for a good long time, then makes his way close and sits. We look at each other. The stillness between us slowly empties of things until it's just stillness.

Seven

Late June, Early July

THERE'S A PLACE I'VE grown to love: Constance Street, on the back side of the hotel across from the gravel parking lot. From here I can see big sky over the city, the sunrises and sunsets and big storms coming in. I can hear the bells at the cathedral on Camp Street ring out over a quiet evening or a weekend morning. I can hear birds chirping and cicadas, see the rough beauty of the Warehouse District spread out in all directions, the different ways that light hits the old brick, glinting windows, peeling paint. Night or day, the bugs attack the moment I step out, but in this one place for some reason, I don't mind.

It's time to fully inhabit my kitchen, make a jambalaya to welcome my partner, Tom. He's coming from Vancouver for a visit. Eight weeks alone in the windowless white room—my workdays spent in the body and solitary mindset of a make-believe orangutan, the rest of my time in solitary wandering—what will it be like to share again?

The moment Tom arrives, we're out the door and into the city. I wonder if it will intrigue or overwhelm him, disgust or enchant? We buy hats at Meyer the Hatter, then head for the Quarter. There's the cops on Canal Street, tossing a pickpocket into a van. There's a waiter rushing by us on his way to work, eating ice cream right out of the tub with a silver spoon. There's a dancing trombone player, a woman pushing a baby carriage full of crap, with a cross sticking out of it and a sign on it that warns "The End is Near." We walk and walk.

Back on the hotel patio Elijah runs to see me and stops, seeing Tom. Tom introduces himself. Elijah goes away and returns a few moments later with the tiniest fern frond.

"If you want to kill something like this," he says to Tom, holding up the fern frond, "you need something like *this*." He holds up the same fern frond, and gives it to Tom.

Another day we walk thirty blocks of Magazine Street, share a roast beef po' boy sandwich and super-thin onion rings at Mahoney's. Another day, we take the streetcar out to the cemeteries and an unholy storm lets loose. We take refuge with two other couples on the back porch of the Sacred Grounds Coffee Shop and Voodoo Emporium, looking out through the chain link fence to the tombs. Thunder crashes, forked lightning fills the sky, the rain pounds down, and the ground quickly saturates and floods.

Back at the hotel, Elijah runs to greet us, "Hullo, my good friends!"

He's wearing a Super Mario costume. Red overalls, yellow buttons, electric-blue sleeves, a red hat with a big white M on it. His father says they ordered it online, Elijah hasn't taken it off for two days. He shows us his imaginary computer games, tracing their progress in the air with his hands—Bad Piggies, Angry Bird, Super Mario. He races from one side of the table to the other, the games taking up more and more space in the air. We clap and "hooray!" the wins.

"Okay!" says Elijah. "Next level!"

Another day we're at Lafitte's Blacksmith Shop, open as a bar since 1772. It's late afternoon, the candles aren't lit yet. Lafitte's doesn't use electric light. There's an artist painting outside across the street. He finishes his work and turns the painting on its easel for passersby to see. He comes to chat with us through the open window. Horse-drawn carriage tours arrive, a waiter rushes to them to get take-out cocktail orders. The painter tells us about a country club where we can get nude with the locals if we wish. Not at all something we'd asked about, but thoughtful of him to offer, I guess. After he leaves, I go round the room taking pictures of bricks, baseboards, an inexplicable light switch. I wonder: is New Orleans reaching Tom? or not really?

In Jackson Square, the All Stars are playing with their beat-up horns. They have a jester with them today, an old fellow in a gold jacket with a smoke hanging out of his mouth. His routine involves a golf club and a handsaw and whatever occurs to him to do with them. Every so often the band leader feigns getting fed up with his scene-stealing shenanigans and chases the old guy round the park bench. At Fritzel's Jazz Bar a "stride jazz" piano player gives a lecture recital to a teachers' convention. When it's over, the place empties, and the bartender turns up the volume on the tv, watching carefully as a man on screen crafts a fern frond out of paper. On our way back up Royal, there's a guy in the middle of the street giving hell on his washboard vest with two big soup spoons. It's kind of magnificent.

"That's the same guy," says Tom.

"Same guy as what?"

"Same guy who was delivering ice to Lafitte's three hours ago," Tom says.

Back at the hotel, Elijah has a tiny dolly who he says will wear a helmet when she rides a bicycle.

"You are my true good friends," he says. He looks intently from one to the other of us, then shows us his computer games, huge in the air, running all the way from one end of the patio to the other. When his father calls him to come, he bursts into tears.

Upstairs in the windowless white room, I'm unsettled and cranky.

What made Elijah cry? And then: is it really such a good idea to be making friends with such a sensitive little kid who I'm going to have say goodbye to when either I or he and his parents leave? I turn to Tom, and not very pleasantly ask him about the washboard-playing ice-delivery man,

"How could you notice and remember him? Why didn't I?"

"I dunno," shrugs Tom. "Maybe you were too busy taking pictures of bricks."

❖ ❖ ❖

Another day we make our way to the Historic New Orleans Collection on Royal Street, a gem of a private museum. If you didn't know it was there, you'd miss it. Like many other places we've heard about in the Quarter, a simple doorway opens into a grand two-story house with inner courtyard and something like a ballroom. We follow the history of New Orleans from room to room, everything from original ship logs from the 1700s to documents and letters surrounding the Louisiana Purchase to something that chills me to the bone: a newspaper ad from the 1800s listing the names and qualities of individual slaves on auction one particular Saturday. I begin to piece together in my mind the city's history: land of the Chitimacha, founded as La Nouvelle-Orléans in 1718 by the French, ceded to the Spanish in 1763, back to the French in 1801, sold to the United States in 1803 by Napoleon (the Louisiana Purchase), Battle of New Orleans 1815 . . . I've never been one for facts and figures but in my desire to understand the city, they become interesting.

I taste my first Sazerac and marvel: it's true. You can actually fall in love with a cocktail. We find Frenchmen Street and the heart of the music scene. It irks me that I didn't find it sooner, but I wouldn't have gone traipsing alone after dark. One night we finally stroll

Bourbon Street, past the girlie shows and mayhem of tourists drunk on drinks with names like Hurricanes and Swamp Water and Hand Grenades. Another evening at the DBA on Frenchmen it's the Treme Brass Band, another evening at Snug Harbour it's Delfeayo Marsalis and his Uptown Jazz Orchestra. The spaces are tiny and unpretentious, the music a no-bullshit lift-off to another world. Another evening, at Preservation Hall on Saint Peter Street, we cram into a decrepit room with a hundred other people to listen to five guys on horns blow the roof off the place. Wending our way back up Bourbon, the party is wilder than ever, there's a guy passed out against a wall wearing a stars-and-stripes T-shirt, cops on horseback moving in. I understand now why the lawyer I first saw on Nola TV two months ago keeps showing up a dozen times a night to warn us,

"They're gonna take your cellphone, they're gonna take your wallet, they're gonna take everything you have, and you won't have a friend in the world! So keep my number in your pocket, as close to you as you can!"

One morning we're standing out back of the hotel on Constance Street, drinking coffee in the morning light. There's an army of ants, a literal army, clambering up the wall to an open brick space where we rest our coffee cups. My cellphone rings, I see from the number it's our friend Jimmy at home. Jimmy lives across the street from us, with his dear doggie Lotte, who I adore. I've kept in regular touch with family and several friends at home since I got here, and phoned Jimmy every few weeks. But it's surprising for him to call me.

"Hello?"

"Karin, it's Jimmy. Lotte . . . is gone."

I burst into tears, and as Jimmy and I sob together over the phone and Tom keeps asking what, what, what?, it seems that the distance between home so far away and me here in New Orleans collapses completely for the first time. I am both places at once, in Jimmy's apartment sobbing with him over the loss of Lotte and here, now, on Constance Street, fingering the army of ants climbing round my coffee cup as I listen to Jimmy tell the story of Lotte's passing. It's a heart-breaking loss, dear Lotte with her soul-searing eyes. I can't imagine that I'll never see her again. I can't imagine the pain for my friend Jimmy. What I can't know now, but will later, is how right it is that I am standing exactly where I am standing to hear this sad news, and how deeply I will remember it.

Later that day, Elijah gets a new bike and pushes it proudly out to show us, but he can't ride it. There's no air in the tires. For the next few nights when we come back late from somewhere, we find it still leaning by the stairwell. The tires pinch easily between my fingers when I test them. For the first two days my heart breaks for him, then I'm just angry.

❖　❖　❖

The fourth of July will be my birthday, and as far as I can recall, the first full birthday I've spent in the United States since I was a child in Baltimore. I remember a party, I may have been four or five. When the candles were lit and everyone began to sing, I ran and hid in the neighbors' yard. I didn't like being looked at, much less sung to. I remember sitting on the pavement of Stoneleigh Court, etching the American flag into the asphalt with a white stone, drawing stars and stripes over and over. No idea that painting would years later become a significant part of my life, and I'd eventually even paint with orangutans. That I'd grow up to make my living being looked at. I haven't drawn or painted a thing in Nola. I have paper with me, pencils, brushes, paint. The windowless white room doesn't offer itself that way, I don't know why.

One day we take the streetcar and the bus to Oak Street Village and wander into a consignment shop. We press through overstuffed racks of clothes following the smell of cigarette smoke, find a woman who introduces herself as Miss K at the back of the store behind her piled-high desk and ashtray. She's a vision in baby-blue silk, a great cream hat with a pink ribbon, ruby-red lipstick, blue eyeshadow, and lacquered nails.

"Welcome! Welcome!" beams Miss K. "Please, make yourselves at home! Everything in the front of the store is on sale, everything in the back is ninety percent off!"

We press through to another room packed with clothes, begin perusing. Despite the amount of merchandise, everything is nicely hung and organized, there's some good pieces. The dressing room is a graciously appointed Blanche Dubois-esque boudoir. I see what Miss K has cleverly done with her "ninety percent off": she's booted up the non-sale price of a garment to fifty-nine dollars. Move the decimal point to the left and you feel like you're getting a really good deal. I find a sweet dress, a pair of leggings, a summer shirt.

"Oh!" says Miss K, glowing. Her cigarette burns long in the ashtray while she carefully writes me a receipt. "These will look stunning on you!"

I watch her, try to memorize every detail. How old might she be . . . seventies? eighties? There's something truly grand and beautiful about her. Holed up at the back of this shop, making a living with style and enthusiasm, making me who's about to turn fifty-two feel good. In ten or twenty or thirty years, will I be able to greet the world like Miss K?

On the fourth of July, my birthday, we ride the St. Charles Streetcar up to Audubon Park and stroll the half-mile through the trees to the zoo. Casey takes one look at Tom, puts his hand gently but firmly on a hanging tire, and keeps it there. It's a short visit.

We head back to Oak Street and Squeal Barbecue. Time for a good old-fashioned Southern meal: ribs, corn bread, coleslaw, and potato salad. We sit outside where the smoke from the smoker wafts over and chokes us now and again, but it's nice to be on the patio, there's no one here but us. A father arrives with his daughter, picks a table further down. She's about four, wearing a pretty blue dress, and doesn't want to sit nicely in a chair and behave herself. She'd rather get down on the garden sidewalk with her chalk and do some drawing. So she does.

Eight

July

TOM LEAVES, AND I keep working. With the ever-rising heat and daily storms and mosquitoes and stinging bugs and biting spiders and long hours and the physical demands of playing a mature male orangutan, it becomes even more difficult. One day on the ride home, there's a dead alligator on the highway. My driver, born and bred in Louisiana, doesn't leap out of his seat. I do. I shouldn't be surprised. Alligators and a host of other frightening creatures have been stalking our location for weeks.

I learn the difference between a swamp and a bayou, and that there are armadillos here. I learn that the trees on the patio are crape myrtle, not lilacs as I thought. As it gets hotter, birds arrive by the hundreds to take up residence in them each night. Hundreds. Chirping.

I learn from the morning news that we are happily down in the number of people struck by lightning this year: only nineteen. I learn that a woman inside a convenience store in Houma was number nineteen. A convenience store. *Inside.*

On a day off, too exhausted for a big explore, I stumble down the block to the Ogden Museum of Southern Art to see an exhibit of Eudora Welty's photographs. She was a photographer before she was a writer and captured the faces of people up and down the Mississippi. Before I even reach the exhibit, I'm taken by an exhibit of banners by school children in Orleans Parish, then another exhibit of photographs from the Ogden Museum collection entitled "Into the Light." On the wall, a written piece by the gallery curator Richard McCabe tells us that it was Eudora Welty who popularized the phrase "a sense of place" and that,

"In the South, place refers to both a geographic location and a state of mind."

For some reason, this stops me cold. I don't yet know why. What I do know is, the moment I arrived in New Orleans a question came into my mind: why am I going to miss this place so much when I leave it? Because I knew immediately, without anything except the sense of landing on another planet, that I would.

I get on the bus up Magazine to go for groceries. There's a police car parked beside a basketball court I've passed two dozen times. It takes me a moment before I remember the news item on tv two days ago. Almost every day the news begins with a list of yesterday or last night's crimes. Tomorrow it will be the beating deaths with baseball bats of tourists in the lower Garden District, not far from where I live. The next day it will be the disappearance of a little girl in a sparkly green dress. Two days ago, it was a police officer run down in the line of duty. Today, like any other day, the kids are out on the basketball court playing ball. The police officer's car parked beside them—where he left it before he was killed in the line of duty—has almost completely disappeared under mounds of floral tributes.

Elijah finally gets air in his bike tires and can ride it. We visit every evening: he brings me a flower and shows me one of his computer games in the air with his hands. I learn that for the Field of Dreams level in Bad Piggies, all we need is one kingpin, ten blocks, a helicopter propeller, one engine, one wheel, and one tire. With these our pigs can get all the stars and proceed to the next sandbox. Elijah dances from one end of the patio to the other, collecting invisible stars,

"They got that star, they got that star, they got that star, they got that star—yay!" shouts Elijah, clapping his hands. "We go to the next sandbox!"

"What's the next sandbox?" I ask.

"It's called, 'When Pigs Fly.'"

"What do we need for that?"

Elijah thinks hard for a moment. Finally, "just each other," he says. "And other pigs to help."

Edgar the security guard gets a new job and leaves. The new security guard invites me to try the sausages at his family grocery near City Park, where he was stacking boxes for his grandfather when he was nine years old. The water coming out of the bathroom faucet in my room begins to smell, quite literally, like shit. A puppet maker in residence at the Contemporary Arts Center down the block begins to fill the window of her studio with puppets. She'll build a hundred of them before summer is through. On a Saturday evening I stroll Canal Street, see a big purple party bus cruising two blocks one way, two blocks the other, then back again. The lower parts of the passenger windows are covered with black paper. Just visible above the black paper are the bouncing heads of a bus full of toddlers, not a kid over the age of five, jumping on their seats with the pounding music. A few of them suck soothers.

At work I have heat stroke for the second time, break a tooth, forget about it, remember it, get sent to a dentist, go off solid food for five days and keep working while I wait for a root canal, get a root canal, and go right back to work an hour later without painkillers so I can concentrate on being an orangutan clambering the side of a hill three stories above ground. A frog takes up residence under my trailer on set until the pain goes away. No joke: the day the pain leaves, so does the frog.

On a Sunday evening, Elijah rides a luggage cart to bring me my flower, he and his mom and dad are heading upstairs for the next load. They've been here a year, they leave tomorrow. I watch them fill their U-Haul parked on Constance Street to the bursting point. The next night they cram more stuff in, and it's time to go. I run upstairs to get a gift for Elijah, a print of one of my paintings I think he'll like.

Then: I stop. Put the gift down. I think: how selfish of me to hold on to him in this way. Let him carry on, let our brief friendship fade into memory.

Downstairs, Elijah steps towards me and back, towards me and back. Finally, I bend down and we hug each other, for the first and last time.

He raises his hand, makes his fingers move like a puppet animal talking, "Um, bye-bye and hugs and kisses to you."

"Hugs and kisses to you too, Elijah."

"You have to wave bye-bye too," he says, "like this . . ."

So I do. Elijah smiles big, runs to the car, and hops in. The back end of the U-Haul bumps down the cobblestones of Constance Street, turns left onto Julia, and they're gone. Back upstairs in the windowless white room, Elijah's dried flower gifts are everywhere. I look at the print of the painting he didn't get. It's the first time in my life I've stopped myself from giving someone a gift. And while I couldn't say why, I know it's a sea-change moment, and one for the better. I gather my hoops and for the first time in weeks, take them down to the tennis court and spin spin spin them under the birds chirping in the crape myrtle trees under the starry sky.

❖ ❖ ❖

Two and a half months into my time here, I finally feel ready to join the tourists. There's less than a dozen of us on the bus to the Creole Laura Plantation. Our guide Sylvester gives, while driving, what I can only describe as a beat-poet spoken-word performance of the history of New Orleans all the way out and back. I won't remember much about the Laura Plantation later, but I'll remember the drive through sugar cane fields and Sylvester and some of what he taught us. That Creole houses were the pretty-colored ones, and bringing a pineapple to someone's home the best gift. That a Southern gentlewoman would never consume alcohol from a glass in front of her husband but she could eat a cherry charger, a bowlful of sherry-soaked fruit. That the longer your knives and forks were the richer you were and that a Creole place setting turned the utensils face to the table. That an alley of oak trees leading from the river to the porch was air conditioning.

Another day I go on a Swamp Tour to Jean Lafitte Park. Before we're even in the boat, a couple of ladies take pictures of each other straddling the ceramic alligator at the gate. This should be my first clue to what's ahead. The tour starts benignly enough, a lovely float down the bayou. Then the Lafitte Park guide digs into what he calls the last of his lunch and starts firing marshmallows overboard. The alligators start to show up, well, like alligators to a marshmallow toss. When everyone's got their fill of pictures and we've scrounged up one finger of bayou and down another rousting every alligator we can, our guide whips open a closet on the boat and poof! Holds up a live baby alligator.

After the screaming stops, he tapes the alligator's jaws shut with black duct tape and hands the little fellow to the person beside him,

"Pass him on down, take as many pictures as you like!"

He cranks up the Zydeco music for the float back and leaves us to it. I can't believe what I'm seeing. One big man cringing as the alligator passes to him, then a boy practically choking it to death, then a woman posing amorously with the baby alligator for a picture.

I ask our guide, "Um—is this baby an alligator rescue? or—?"

He gives me a bad-smell face. "An alligator what?"

Between workdays and bus-tour days I go to visit Casey the gorilla. He sees me, I greet him with a nod, he makes his way to his same rock shelf perch with the overhanging shade, I sit on the same bench in the shade of a tree. We look at each other in silence. Every once in a while, I sip from my water bottle or pull out a fresh frozen handkerchief from my thermos bag to mop at the sweat, sometimes Casey goes off briefly to get a leafy twig, brings it back to slowly chew at. We watch visitors come, rarely stay more than five minutes, move along. One of us may notice a tiny darting lizard or a bird flitting by or consider the pace of afternoon storm clouds gathering above us. We look back to each other. By late July, we've spent more than a dozen afternoons like this. I have to laugh at myself, at how I wondered two months ago where this friendship was heading. From all outward appearances, to the same place it began. Silence. Stillness. Looking at each other. And, as I also felt when we first met, that whatever Casey's giving me is something I came on this journey to get, I would say now that this has proven true. But what it is exactly, I can't name it.

I continue hooping on the tennis court most evenings after everyone has gone to bed, still exploring a choreography of sorts, putting phrases of hooping movements together, but there've been no more "ah hah" moments that take me to a next level. When I find this frustrating, I remind myself to let it go, relax back into my lack of skill with hooping, its lack of importance in my life. It's uncanny how, whenever I do this, the hoops begin to spin more easily again, and I can just breathe and rest, riding their circling-to-nowhere spirals of energy.

One day I take the Hurricane Katrina bus tour out to Lake Pontchartrain and the levees, to the neighborhoods hardest hit and still recovering, other neighborhoods completely destroyed. Some places there's just street signs on corners, the remnants of a house foundation or sidewalk barely visible in the overgrowth. It's jaw-dropping to see how much remains of the damage, to imagine the surge of Pontchartrain into the city, the people lost, the people who barely made it out. Our guide was one of them, neighbors around him among the lost. He says his son was one of the many who got stuck but found a way to help others: when the waters trapped him on his roof he dove in, swam to the mall down the block where there was a hardware store, was pleased to see that the boat he'd seen parked in front of it two days earlier was still there and floating. So he took the boat and began driving around the neighborhood, ferrying people to rescue on higher ground. His son got twenty-nine people out before he ran out of gas, our driver says.

In Gentilly and the Ninth Ward I take pictures of house after house, what's left of them eight years later, a chilling "X" still on a wall, a window, a door. Our bus is quiet. We're all here for different reasons. One lady, clutching tissues, hasn't been back since Katrina, until today. She thought a public bus tour would be easier, give her a bit more distance, than driving in with friends. Another young woman who lives somewhere else lost her aunt to Katrina and has been back once but wants to see how things are coming along in the neighborhood her aunt lived in. They aren't, she says.

The truth is, eight years later, many parts of New Orleans still aren't recovered. While I've heard this and seen evidence of it—the full city blocks of abandoned high-rises downtown—and I know about the schools, half of them gone, and the food deserts—whole neighborhoods with not even a basic grocery store for miles and unless you own a car no way to get there—it's one thing to hear about it. Quite another to see.

On a Sunday morning, I hop a cab into Treme to Saint Augustine's Church. The moment I step through the door, the full-on gospel singing hits me and I'm fishing for Kleenex. The next evening I'm on Frenchmen Street by myself for the first time, sipping my first Nola mojito at a patio bar, a sixteen-piece big band inside the restaurant blowing the roof off the place. Whether I have my camera with me or not, the pictures continue to appear, sear into memory: four young girls in sparkly pink birthday crowns, riding the bus together holding hands. A group of construction workers squatting on the ground, sharing the six-inch strip of shade beside a car to eat lunch. An infestation of crazy ants behind the hotel devouring an enormous grasshopper. A night stroll up Decatur Street, where every doorway holds . . . something.

◆　◆　◆

The first of August: I learn that I'm leaving in two weeks. I've looked forward to returning home to Vancouver, so my reaction astonishes me: I feel . . . bereft.

Nine

August Farewell

A BACKGROUND PERFORMER ON OUR film who I've never met, who's an artist, gives me a stunning charcoal drawing of an orangutan. The woman who's shared my actor's journey with me as my stand-in gives me a stunning charcoal scarf. She's knitted it while she watched and waited. The daughter of another friend I've made on set gives me drawings and a dozen homemade chocolate-chip cookies.

I take the streetcar up to my library to return two books. I feel a bit sheepish: they're the only books I've taken out. Walking the six blocks from St. Charles to my favorite Café Luna on Magazine, my clothes stick to me and I've given up mopping sweat. Lizards dart over my shoes. Thunder rumbles, next storm coming in.

The weekly farmers' market is shutting down by the time I arrive, but the lady who sits on the street corner knitting baby hats shaped like vegetable tops is still there. I haven't seen her in a month. She asks what I've learned about her city since we last met. The conversation lasts half an hour. She knits under her sun umbrella while I pour sweat in the noonday sun.

"Are you going to brass mass at Saint A's tomorrow?" she asks.

Her assumption that I know what she's talking about—and I

do—makes me happy.

"Yes, I am. And next week I go home."

"Come find me the next time you're in Nola," she says.

"Well. That may be a long time."

"That's okay," she says. "I'll be here."

In PJ's Coffee they're playing Sinatra's "One for my baby, one more for the road." Waiting for my coffee, I watch a young Asian girl at a table as she bends over a notebook practicing her handwriting. In green pen, huge letters, she writes:

I WILL CARE FOR YOU ALWAYS.

Outside, the bells ring at the cathedral and tiny birds dance round me begging for sesame seeds. Black clouds appear overhead, thunder rumbles. I race back to the hotel, watch for a storm that never comes. Later, out taking pictures, I dart between catering trucks setting up tables down three blocks of Julia Street: tonight is White Linen Night. In a few hours, thousands of people wearing white linen will stroll from gallery to gallery in the Warehouse District, listening to music and dining in the middle of the street.

In a designer clothing and furniture gallery, I wind up in another hour-long conversation about Nola with the woman who runs the place. When she hears what I've been photographing, the images in the city that have struck me, she urges me to submit an exhibit proposal to two galleries down the block, curators she knows well who she says would want to know about this. I say I'd never presume to present New Orleans to New Orleanians, it's just my personal journey through it.

"Yes," she says. "Exactly."

An hour later I'm taking pictures of a yellow dragonfly on peeling yellow paint on a rusty post in a parking lot. The parking lot attendant is bored, waiting for the onslaught of White Linen Night parkers.

"I hate this city," he says. "Then I love it. Then I hate it again."

As dusk falls, I join the throngs in white linen on Julia Street. I have no white clothes to wear so I slip down the shadow of buildings in my red and blue, hiding behind my camera.

The next morning the woman I met yesterday at the gallery is on the tv news. It seems that shortly after I left, a van pulled up and two men jumped out. They ripped down a rainbow flag belonging to a gay couple who live above her shop, spray-painted the wall of her gallery with homophobic slurs, hopped back in their van, and took off. It was over, she tells the tv news reporter, before she knew it.

I get a cab to Saint Augustine's in Treme. When I went to mass last week, I was turned down by two cab drivers before a third would take me there. It puzzled me, still does. The cabbie who picks me up this week only asks, as he's dropping me off,

"How you plan on leaving?"

I smile at him and mean it, "I'll be fine."

The brass mass this week is in honor of Louis Armstrong's birthday. Last week, the paper fans on popsicle sticks handed out at the door—Saint Augustine's doesn't have air conditioning—were courtesy of a funeral home, and throughout the mass I watched their ads for cremation services flapping. This week there's a beaming picture of Satchmo, Louis Armstrong, on the fans. Much cheerier. The service hasn't started but the choir and horns are already going balls-to-the-wall as I walk in, the congregation on their feet dancing and clapping. The priest's sermon this morning is about joy.

"How many of you let yourselves," he asks us, arms flung wide, "when a moment of joy comes along to just be *in* it?"

The brass mass crescendos to an all-out jam session, every horn gets its day. At the last moment, a well-known singer steps from a sanctuary door to roars of applause and takes the show home at the top of her lungs. Musicians parade through the congregation, parasols snap open, and hankies wave as people join in to second line out the door and into the street.

I pull a blue bandana from my purse and dance along too. In the street another band is waiting, and another, and another, and another, and another. We second line to Rampart and up past Louis Armstrong Park, back down Rampart to Esplanade, down Esplanade to Frenchmen, where three months ago on Mother's Day nineteen people were gunned down in a second line parade just like ours.

There's hundreds of us, as diverse a crowd of people as I first danced with in the second line parade I joined at Jazz Fest—young and old, fat and thin, black and white and olive-skinned and tanned and pale and freckled, some people being pushed along in wheelchairs, some step-touching carefully, leaning on their canes, children who just learned to walk, tottering along. I dance forward with one band, fall back to join another, another, another. The police hover round us, and I know now that what happened on Mother's Day could happen again any time here but the point in Nola seems to be: dance anyway. Dance *through*.

Back in the windowless white room hours later, I collapse on the bed and turn on the tv. The evening news is just beginning. There's a five-second clip of the parade to start the show. Of all those bands, six blocks of hundreds of dancing people—the five-second clip on the news is of one dancing person, beaming with joy . . . me.

❖　❖　❖

On Monday I get my new tooth, the dentist high-fives and hugs me. Tuesday in the newspaper headlines: an extreme heat advisory and a shooting in Marigny yesterday. The very same corner I ate lunch, after the parade.

In the windowless white room, I begin to pack and let go of things I can't take home, as joyfully as possible. Yoga mat, weights, glow-in-the-dark hula hoops, so many other collected things. Elijah's dried flower gifts, scattered everywhere.

In the evening I tune my iPod to Astor Piazzolla's "Maria de Buenos Aires," and for the first time ever stroll out into the dark listening to music. The heat at ten o'clock is still suffocating, but somehow in the last few days I've come to accept it less as a vice grip, more an affectionate embrace. Walking past walls and windows and doors and peeling paint and rotting wood and all else in my neighborhood that has grown so familiar, the bereft feeling returns. Like the bricks, the very fabric of this city, has reached into me.

Turning back up Constance Street from Julia, I stop beside one of the bright blue side doors of the Children's Museum at the beginning of the block. I hold my hands up to the brick wall, my palms open to it but a few inches away, not touching. The cumulative heat of the day is still palpable, almost a vibration, a pulsing from the bricks that brushes gently against my palms. I close my eyes and stand there, soaking it in. After a few minutes I carry on up the block, past the gravel parking lot and the side door entrance where I stand every morning with my coffee, up to Saint Joseph Street and left to the hotel's main entrance, the only way in at night.

Back in the windowless white room I lie awake, remembering a conversation I had with a friend on the film set a few weeks ago. He's a man born and bred in Louisiana and a passionate New Orleanian. He was telling me about the "Bud Light Zone" during the recent Super Bowl. How Bud Light wanted it to be a certain size, Nola didn't. So Bud Light didn't get the French Quarter as they'd wished, then the area they did get was further and further reduced. New Orleans was going to be New Orleans or forget your Super Bowl. My friend has been a fountain of helpful information for my explorations. I've asked him lots of questions and bounced thoughts about the city around with him the past few months. We've talked of the city's obvious charms, the music and food and etcetera. But unpleasant stuff too—the blocks of deserted high-rises, Katrina, the murders, the terrible daily accidents on the roads.

He asked me, "Do you think if New Orleans cleaned up it would be a better place?"

I thought about it for maybe a second. "Of course not. It wouldn't be New Orleans."

Two days ago we were talking Nola again, laughing about me winding up on the news with a sweat-soaked bandana on my head. He suddenly turned serious and said,

"Thank you for appreciating my city in all that it is. Not just its romantic image."

What struck me most about his remark was: how deeply he meant this.

❖   ❖   ❖

A last day to do favorite things. I ride the St. Charles Streetcar to Audubon Park, walk along the bayou. Visit Casey. When I arrive, he appears to be doing some kind of gorilla yoga, lying on his back with one leg in the air, his fingers gently stretching the leg towards his chest. He notices me, takes an unusual amount of time making his way to the shaded area on his favorite rock shelf. He looks at me, long and hard. I suddenly realize: he knows I've come with something to say. I'd hoped so much to drift here in his company for a while, one last afternoon together in silence and stillness. But the way he's studying me, the question in his eyes, his alert waiting . . . he needs me to tell him, right now.

"Casey," I begin. It's surprisingly difficult to say. "Casey . . . I have to go home now. I live far away, and I don't know if I'll see you again.

Thank you for . . . being my friend."

Casey leans forward, his head cocked to one side, squinting at me. A beat. Then, though I can't explain why, I see it: he understands. He sniffs, shakes his head slightly back and forth, looks to the rock overhang above him.

"Casey? I'm leaving now."

He shakes his head slightly back and forth again, keeps staring upward.

"Casey?"

He shakes his head once more, this time more slowly, a very clear and deliberate, No.

Suddenly one of the female gorillas comes running from a corner of the yard carrying a six- foot length of browse, really a small tree. She storms to the top of the rock above Casey and hurls it at me.

"Holy shit!" says a man just arriving beside me.

The female gorilla growls and plants herself, staring at me. Her message is clear: go the hell away.

In spite of her, I try one more time, "Casey? Could you just—look at me?"

He stares determinedly at the rock hang overhead, completely still. As I wave goodbye, he doesn't budge, doesn't look. I check back over my shoulder three times on my way down the path. A proud, glorious silverback gorilla, he holds his goodbye, fiercely.

On the #11 bus back down Magazine, a man gets on carrying a great green flowered Mardi Gras ornament, the kind you might bounce and wave in a second line parade. He's wearing a Superman T-shirt. It's the very same fellow who was a riding a toy stuffed horse on the St. Charles Streetcar a few months ago.

"That's a beautiful baton you have," I say. "May I take your picture?"

He grins and poses with it. After the picture he fishes into the top end of the baton and wrestles something out of it,

"For you!" he says. "Special present!"

He tosses it to me: a great green silk flower.

Back in the windowless white room, now empty of all traces of my presence in it these past four months, I wrap the flower carefully for the trip home.

Ten

Hooping Home

HAVING REPACKED MY SUITCASE three times this week further editing my belongings, I'm now sprawled on the floor of the train station unceremoniously chucking things from it into a cardboard box. According to Amtrak it's twenty-five pounds overweight, there's a fifty-pound limit. There's a good reason for this that I'm sheepish to admit even to myself: all those souvenir shops on Decatur Street in the Quarter that I recoiled from when I first arrived? Well, they got me in the end. My suitcase is filled to bursting with multiples of every New Orleans souvenir you could wish for—mugs, spoon rests, T-shirts, dish towels, cajun spice mix, pot holders, fridge magnets, plates, baseball caps, shopping totes, you name it—gifts for at least a dozen friends and family for sure, but a goodly number of souvenirs for myself too. I keep the treasured souvenirs in my suitcase that will come with me in the roomette, chuck less valued things into the cardboard box that will travel in the luggage car. Arriving passengers step round me as you might a homeless person rearranging the contents of their shopping cart. Blanket, half empty bottle of shampoo, yesterday's dirty clothes. The ticket agent watches closely as I reweigh the suitcase: forty-nine pounds. Thank God.

There were no roomettes available on the train they call The City of New Orleans back to Chicago or The Empire Builder from Chicago to Seattle, so the film production is sending me home a longer way round, on the Sunset Limited west to Los Angeles, then north to Seattle on The Coast Starlight. While the trip will be much longer, it delights me to be travelling a full circle round a large part of the country, hooping my way home as it were. It seems appropriate. As the train pulls out of the station and I wave farewell to New Orleans, I remember the couple I travelled down with. The couple who met, married, and bought a house on three Friday the thirteenths. I wonder, where are they now?

Late morning in the dome car, somewhere in Louisiana between New Iberia and Lafayette. Storm after storm rolls over us. A young Japanese woman sits reading, her feet in white toe socks up on the cocktail ledge. She glances over at me now and then as if about to speak, then either changes her mind or is too shy.

At lunch in the dining car the steward sits me with three M's: a Michael, a Mary, and Masito, the girl with the white toe socks. She is indeed very shy and tells us in a tiny voice that she is on her way across America to study at a placed called

"Simon Fraser University in Vancouver British Columbia Ca-na-da."

When I tell her I'm from Vancouver, Masito lights up as if she's met someone from the promised land. She orders exactly what I do, a veggie burger with Swiss cheese.

Michael introduces himself as a professional from Houston and asks, "You speak French up there in Columbia?"

"*British* Columbia," I answer. "And . . . no."

We move in and out of storms all afternoon through eastern Louisiana. I cuddle at the window in my roomette, drifting. A few times I stand up and look into a mirror above the little sink. Face to face with myself as just myself for the first time in months. No more inner orangutan needed as the job—for the moment—is done. It's disconcerting.

At dinner in the dining car the steward sits me with three T's: Tina and her two grown sons, Tommy and Tony. If I get another alliteratively named group of dining companions, I'll grow suspicious. I make the mistake of answering honestly when Tina asks me what I do for a living. She whips out her camera.

"Gimme a picture of you so I can show it to my friends and tell them *I know her!* And tell me every single thing you been in, maybe I seen it!"

New Orleans has turned me into a blunter person, "But you *don't* know me," I say. "Forget the picture. Let's talk about something else."

If I hurt her feelings, she doesn't show it and rattles off her list of wished-for encounters with stars. Top of the list and for different reasons: Emeril and Paula Dean. Her sons stay silent, eating their twin plates of meat. Finally, Miss Heather who runs the dining car rescues me,

"There's a beautiful sunset on the other side of the train."

I hop across the aisle and am seconds late to grab it as I fish for my camera, the sun a great glowing red fireball landing on the horizon, hovering brilliantly for a moment, then it's gone.

We arrive in San Antonio, Texas, at midnight, and at this ungodly hour we're set loose for three hours to explore the town. People scatter in all directions, some to find a drink on the River Walk half a mile from here, some to find the Alamo. I walk a few dark blocks past lit-up palm trees, turn onto a busier street lined with bars, music pounding into the street. I think of stepping into one, but none look welcoming like Nola, and then I remember Atlanta. Back to the train or find the Alamo? I see a couple from our train heading under the freeway overpass into the city and run to catch up with them. Find the Alamo!

❖   ❖   ❖

In the morning I wake to a grand desert and a whimsical gathering of six goats below my window. The desert continues for hours and hours, scruffy hills form, and great cracks in the earth. Closer to El Paso the orchards of fruit trees begin, then the backyard junkyards. I sit alone in my room, cuddled at the window, drifting with the scenery, my mind unusually empty of thoughts. I'm in a between-worlds place, not ready to move on just yet, too soon to process or understand the things I've seen and experienced the last few months, and missing the focus and discipline of inner orangutan solitude that my job required. Who am I now? It makes me laugh: without my solitary inner orangutan on board, I don't really want to meet or talk to anybody.

After spending the whole day in my roomette, finally by evening I'm starving. Miss Heather in the dining car is most perceptive: she sits me at a table with a man named Jack, and doesn't cram two more people in with us as is generally the rule. Jack is an architect, he's on his way to San Luis Obispo. Later I won't remember how the conversation took off or any details of it, but for the next four or five magic hours, Jack and I talk up a storm. About New Orleans and other cities, buildings and bricks and life and love and learning of all kinds. When Miss Heather finally has to close the dining car, we retreat to the bar car where at some time long past midnight when we've been the only people left in it for an hour, and not even drinking, the kind bartender finally tells us gently that he needs to go to sleep. Jack and I trade contact information, the only person on my whole journey I've done this with, aside from the people I worked with.

A third full day passes in my roomette, drifting with the scenery outside the window. Stepping off the train in Tucson, Arizona, the air is warm, there's a good breeze. A man with a carved walking stick comes out to pace the platform and sing. I bring out one of my small arm hoops and for the next half hour practice tosses and catches, over-and-under spins. A young man hovers at the fence beside the train platform. All the departing passengers are gone, the ones who will be joining us are lined up inside the station. Why is this young man just standing there? Five minutes before we leave, I get it. He's just come down to look at the train. I can see from the way he hangs at the fence, leaning forward, how he longs to join us. Getting back aboard I can see him from my window. As the Sunset Limited pulls slowly out of the station, passing by him, he leans further over the fence, waving at all of us with both hands. He waves and waves, and from way past the station looking back, I can still see him waving. I imagine him waving after us until we are nothing but a speck in the distance.

◆　◆　◆

We arrive in Los Angeles at dawn. Homeless people sleep in the station, outside the panhandlers descend. A gray light rises behind the palm trees. It's cool and misting, the coolest air I've felt since Jazz Fest in Nola. I put on a jacket for the first time since then. Back in the Amtrak lounge, I sit with a gentleman who tells me he's on the last leg of an eleven-day journey to visit all his old army buddies before they die. He tells me of his journey from San José to San Francisco, to Denver, to Chicago, to Washington, to Miami, to New Orleans. He tells me which buddies he saw where and only chokes back tears once, early in his story. It was in Denver, where he thought he only had one buddy left there but it turned out there were three, and they had a surprise barbecue in his honor when he came. In the new year he plans another trip, up to Canada and across the prairies in the snow.

"The last time I rode a train across Canada," he says, "it was a steam locomotive. The passageways between the cars frosted over and were freezing cold, but in my bedroom staring out at the snow, it was so warm." He nods and smiles to himself, transported back in time. Which makes me smile too.

Boarding the Coast Starlight for the last leg of my journey home, I'm starting to feel itchy for this ride to be done. Having traveled Vancouver to Los Angeles and back on the Coast Starlight about twenty times for different jobs the past several years, while the scenery will be lovely, I've already seen all thirty-seven hours of it those same twenty times. My sleeping car attendant Jaime is happy to see me again. He remembers me from my first journey on the Coast Starlight years ago. He's still as gently enthusiastic about the journey now as he was back then. I wonder how he does it. As much as I love a train, for myself after seventy-five hours of constant travel so far, the romance of this particular rail journey is wearing thin. All the way up the coast of California I move restlessly from my roomette, to the observation car, to the dining car, to the parlor car, back to my roomette, back to the dining car. I meet no memorable passengers, have no memorable conversations. I tell myself crankily it's because there's no one interesting on this train. Of course, deep inside, I know better. Before going to sleep that night, I ask Jaime to knock and wake me the next morning for the eight-a.m. fresh air break at Klamath Falls, Oregon.

Jaime looks sadly disappointed, "You don't want me to wake you to see the sunrise at Mount Shasta at five? How can you possibly miss that?"

So I promise Jaime I'll wake myself in time for sunrise at Mount Shasta. And to my surprise, the next morning at five a.m. precisely . . . I do. The sunrise is glorious.

❖ ❖ ❖

The sun is setting as we pull into King Street Station in Seattle that evening. I've come full circle. Before continuing home to Vancouver,

I'll stop here to visit my human and orangutan friends at the zoo. I wonder if Melati will turn a cold shoulder as she did last summer when I was gone for two months. If Towan will look at me, or if this is one of those times when he won't. If he has any sense that every moment of my actor's journey, I've called on him in one way or another. If he or Melati or Chinta or Heran or Bela have any clue that their pictures have surrounded me, how thinking of them has grounded me, reminded me what's what in orangutan mind when I've needed it most. I doubt it.

The next morning I'm a bit too excited. I remind myself of my old mantra when coming to see orangutan friends: release expectations. It's needless. Melati comes straight to the window, points at my shoulder bag—open it. She sees the paints, points at them—begin. So I do. Soon Chinta joins us, she taps on the glass—turn the paper so I can see too. Heran comes in from outside, sees me there painting for Melati and Chinta. He gets so excited he starts swinging round the room. Melati and Chinta and I watch him cautiously, wondering where this is heading. Then Melati frowns and bangs on the window at me, Keep Painting. Heran keeps flying round the room, out the door to the outside habitat, back in, around the room again, back out, back in. It will be late afternoon before he finally settles down and cuddles in beside his aunt Chinta, gently grooming her and watching painting over her shoulder.

When I get to the enclosure next door, Towan and his daughter Bela are resting on a platform, visiting with people at the window. The moment Towan sees me, he leaps up and swings down off the platform and starts grabbing at hay. He takes an armload outside and flings it in the air, comes back in for more, takes it outside and flings it in the air, comes back in for more, takes it outside and flings it in the air. He comes back in and swings round and round the indoor habitat, chucking barrels this way and that, giving an orangutan long call loud and long, so loud it can easily be heard through the thick window. Well, well. So he's happy to see me. It takes a while before his excitement winds down, and he and his daughter Bela settle again on the platform, their heads close together and watching as I open my bag and get out the paper and paints. Towan looks deeply into my eyes for a long moment, looks to my lips to read them as I say,

"Hullo, my friend. It's so good to be with you again."

I reach into the pocket of my shirt, pull out the tiny length of straw he gave me as a gift back in April, that I've kept with me this entire journey. I hold it up to show him, grinning. Towan studies it for a moment. Then he looks back to my eyes and the left corner of his lip twitches upward with what I'd swear was the hint of an answering smile. Then it's gone. He sniffs, shrugs, and stares pointedly at the pad of paper in my lap: get on with it. Paint.

Eleven

On Constance

IT'S FOUR YEARS BEFORE I return to New Orleans. I'm flying again so this time I go by air. As the flight takes off from Seattle it's astonishing to think: I'll be there in less than five hours. Not three days. I'm on my way to an Orangutan Species Survival Plan conference. Probably not most people's cup of tea, but as a student of orangutans, I can hardly wait. This is my third conference, so I'll be meeting up with a hundred or more people I know. Quite different from the solitude I travelled in last time.

Since I was last in Nola, among other projects, I've filmed a third movie as my orangutan character. Towan again inspired me throughout. A week after we wrapped, I felt I should go see him immediately. I went, and painted for him on his last afternoon outside in the sun. He died a day later. At the time of his passing, he was the oldest male orangutan in North America. We had six years of a very special friendship. I miss him very much. My friendship with Melati, Chinta, Bela and Heran continues with regular visits. Melati and I paint together for hours a day when I'm there. She chooses all the colors, knocks on the window to tell me when to change them. I've published a children's book, had solo exhibits of my other artwork. But the writings and photographs from my summer in New Orleans have seemed too small and personal a journey to be of interest to anyone beyond myself, so they're filed on a shelf. Sometimes I look at the photographs, and it's funny—I treasure my memories of finding them more than the photographs themselves. I've kept in touch with colleagues from the film, and Jack, my dinner companion on the train. I think of Elijah often, wonder how he is. I've learned that Casey was moved to a zoo in another city so, sadly, he won't be there this time.

Before I know it, the plane is making its descent to Louis Armstrong Airport. It occurs to me that at this point in my trip to Nola four years ago, I'd still be in eastern Washington, just finishing dinner with the couple who met, married, and bought a house on three Friday the thirteenths. As with going to visit my orangutan friends, I've told myself the same thing about this return to Nola: release expectations. It's bound to be different. I considered going back to the windowless white room but then: no. If New Orleans has taught me anything it's to dance forward. Dance *through*.

I hang my head out the window of the cab like a dog all the way into town, inhaling deeply. The hotel is on Tchoupitoulas Street in my old neighborhood, the Warehouse District, and the closer we get the more I feel it: no need to release expectations. The very bricks of the city seem to envelop me in a familiar embrace. For three days before the conference starts, I meander from dawn til dusk, at first alone, then with friends. PJ's Coffee, Rouses Grocery, the St. Charles Streetcar, Audubon Park, my old library, Café Luna on Napoleon, Canal Street, the cemeteries, the Creole Creamery, Saint Augustine's Cathedral, every block of the Quarter, including a wild night's walk up Bourbon Street . . . the where and what seems to matter less than just being in Nola, soaking in it.

When the conference starts, I choose not to move to the hotel where everyone else is staying and taking shuttle buses from there to the zoo. I stay on Tchoupitoulas, and each morning at the coffee shop downstairs, I wait for a paper bag filled with icing sugar and four fresh hot beignets, that I carry carefully onto the #11 bus up Magazine and at coffee break share surreptitiously with a friend from Seattle. The presentations and workshop sessions go from nine to six each day. In the evenings, in different groupings, we fan out to explore. Then I wander alone back to my quiet room on Tchoupitoulas, just breathing in the bricks. I should have realized, even in the midst of an orangutan conference surrounded by friends, Nola would call me to solitude.

I haven't wished to visit the gorillas, there's no point since Casey's not there. But on one of the lunch breaks, a few of us go to see the orangutans. Like Casey, Berani has moved to another zoo, so there's only two orangutans at the moment, Feliz and her daughter Menari— who had her fourth birthday party when I was last here. She's eight now. There's an entirely new exhibit area, a wonderful outdoor habitat that Feliz and Menari seem to delight in. At eight, Menari is a whirling dervish around the great yard while her mother watches patiently. Windows now line one side of the habitat so if they wish, they can come and check out visitors up close. And they do. As soon as we arrive, Feliz comes to the window to investigate. I kneel down and meet her eye to eye. I ask, in words and gestures, if she'd like to see some drawing, and get out my notebook. She hunkers down, arms round her knees, watching closely as I draw a flower. Then: Menari swings in, her hands and face press smack! to the glass. I have no paints with me so I get a lipstick and mascara from my purse and use them to paint the flower, red and black. Menari stares from the flower to my face, the flower to my face, her mouth agape, her forehead scrunched into the window, her hand above it shading her eyes from the sun.

The next day I bring art paper and the tube paints I use to paint with Melati. On the conference lunch break, I race to the orangutans. Menari flies in and plants her face to the window before I've even got there myself. I get out the paper, the paint tubes, begin to paint. She is wide-eyed and riveted, staring at the paper, her lower lip fallen open, her forehead pressed into the window so hard it's squishing her face. I gesture to Feliz to come join us, but she doesn't. Menari and I disappear together into the painting.

Suddenly there's a rush of water from above, and I'm soaking wet. I leap up, what the—? I see Feliz, a slight smirk on her face, putting her hand back in her lap. I look up and see the shower hose head just above me, realize Feliz has a control button on her side of the window. As I'm still looking up, another rush of water, straight into my face. I rub my eyes dry on my sleeve then watch as, even more slowly, Feliz puts her hand back in her lap: yes, painter lady, that was me. I get the message and slip away.

But when I return later in the day, playing hooky from one of the conference presentations because I just can't stop myself going back, Feliz waits for me at the window. When I get out the paints and Menari flies in, Feliz arm-blocks her from joining us. Menari tries this way, that way to maneuver round her mother, but Feliz is calm and fast with her blocking arm and finally, Menari retreats. Fifteen minutes pass, moving paint over paper for Feliz, who watches deeply. Then Menari starts horning in again and her mother sighs and moves off, looking to me as if to say, go ahead. She's all yours.

But Menari doesn't want painting. She's got a devilish twinkle in her eye. She plants her face to the window, clearly wanting my attention, but then darts back six feet, wiggles her head from side to side with a goofy kind of open-mouth face, back to me at the window, away again and another goofy wiggle, this time using her butt too, then she somersaults off to the right, races back, another wiggle, another race to the right, back to face me, another wiggle . . . and finally, I get it. She wants me to *play*. I look to Feliz who shrugs, go for it. The next thing I know Menari and I are racing back and forth on either side of the glass, trying to trick each other which way we're going to run next, sometimes somersaulting (well, I only try the somersault once), sometimes playing hide-and-seek behind posts and sneaking up on and surprising each other, Menari clapping her hands in joy, both of us on all fours wiggling our butts. When a docent arrives and catches us at it, she looks like she might need smelling salts. Seven years knowing orangutans, three films playing one, I've never played like an orangutan, *with* an orangutan, in my life. And, however much I'd hoped for connection with the orangutans four years ago, getting an irreplaceable friend in Casey the gorilla instead, this is the last kind of magic I expected on a return visit. But then: this is Nola.

❖   ❖   ❖

After the conference I have one more day in the city before flying on to New York Comic Con for an event connected to the most recent film. Little did Menari know, but I will soon be quadrupeding orangutan-style for hundreds of fans. She warmed me up good. There's a tropical storm threatening to become a hurricane making its way to New Orleans. As much as I long to stay I'm okay to go, I don't yet feel ready to dance through a hurricane. A last dawn-to-dusk meander takes me and my friends from my first-ever visit to the infamous Café Du Monde, through the Quarter, to Frenchmen and the jazz bars, all the way back up to dinner in the Warehouse District. After farewells I head back out along Julia Street from Tchoupitoulas. There's one place I've hesitated to visit, almost afraid to in case it's not the same, but I have to go there. Alone, in the quiet, in the dark. It's after ten o'clock, hot and still.

Over the past four years if there's one place that's called to me louder than anywhere else, that's transported me to Nola instantly, it's . . . here. This one block of Constance Street, between Julia and Saint Joseph. To my left, the same blue doors in the brick walls. Further up to the right, the same gravel parking lot. Further up to the left, the hotel's side entrance and above that the walls of my windowless white room. I walk slowly up to Saint Joseph, back down to Julia.

There's where I stood every morning with coffee, watching the sun rise over the city, listening to birds chirping, preparing myself for a hard day's work. There's where I stood watching storms come in, or listening for the bells at the cathedral on Camp Street. There's the brick ledge where the ants crawled round my coffee cup the day Jimmy phoned to tell me of Lotte. There's where I said goodbye to Elijah, there's where the U-Haul was parked, where it disappeared round the corner. There's where I stood thinking about all the things I was seeing in my journeys through the city, whatever delightful image I'd most recently caught with my camera. There's where I stood thinking about Casey, the mystery of stillness between us. There's where I stood contemplating the next movements in my hooping choreography, or just feeling them inside me, still circling. There's where I stood holding my hands up to the heat of the bricks on that last August evening, wanting to stand there forever and feeling bereft at the thought of leaving. To this day I've never fully understood. Bereft of what, exactly? A *city*?

I stand for the longest time, then make my way back to the hotel on Tchoupitoulas. By morning, the first bands of wind and rain have arrived and the tv news is all about upcoming flight cancellations. I become more interested in getting to the airport and on a plane than fond farewells. I tell myself I'll be back soon, sooner than four more years, surely. At the airport, just as I'm going through security, everyone's phones—and I do mean *everyone's*—start to blare with emergency alerts. The storm is now a hurricane, and it's coming right at us. For someone who didn't fly for many years and has only recently begun to do so again, getting up in the air doesn't seem the best idea at the moment but neither does staying on the ground. I board my flight, which takes off and ascends like the most terrifying ride at an amusement park. The tailwind gets us to New York forty-five minutes early. All the way there I concentrate on the seatback in front of me, try to imagine a warm brick wall, hold my mind and hands to it.

❖ ❖ ❖

Two and a half years later, I've been many other places but not yet back to New Orleans. A global pandemic hits, we go into lockdown. I won't be going anywhere for a long time. In the first months, living in our little apartment in Vancouver's densely-populated West End, I move cautiously to grocery store and back, for a walk into the park and back. A lot of my time is spent in a three-by-five-foot space in my bedroom, on a Pilates mat. I stopped hooping long ago, not long after I left Nola. I guess it belonged to that time and place. I went back to the gym, lifting weights, cycling, then into a deeper study of the practice of qigong, which I'd begun twenty years earlier but never with steady focus.

In the afternoons on my walks to the park, I phone my friend Jimmy across the street. For the first months we talk every day. To my surprise, I was ready for this lockdown. From what he tells me, it seems Jimmy feels the same. In some strange way we're both treasuring the retreat into solitude. The only thing I truly miss is time with my orangutan friends. Unlike my human friends, I can't Zoom with them. Little do I know that two years later we will still be in pandemic and, aside from when I'm at work on a set or at the grocery store or in the park or with my family, I'll still be standing in practice in the three-by-five-foot space beside my bed.

A year and a bit into the pandemic, I jokingly suggest to Jimmy that we should write a book. Not together. Each to our own writing projects, across the street from each other. Twenty-one weeks later I have a full first draft. Jimmy and I give ourselves a length of time to edit our respective material before handing over to read each other's work. It's not long before I realize: I can't see yet what to do with this story. It needs to be filed away for a time. What to give Jimmy?

I think of my New Orleans story, dig it out, and read it for the first time in seven years. It still seems such a small, personal journey, not worth sharing. I'd titled it "Hooping in Nola." Hooping to where? why? who cares? I go back into qigong practice.

"Qi" means energy. "Gong" means skill, or to work with. At its simplest, the practice could be described as a coming together of physical movement, breath, and mind focus, working with the underlying energy meridians as described in traditional Chinese medicine. It can be practiced in, thankfully, the three-by-five-foot space beside my bed. It's still a full workout: warming up with breath and sometimes vigorous physical practices to activate energy within, then stretches and clearing, then sequences of flowing movement. It's during the flow sequences that qigong sometimes reminds me of hula hooping. Only without the hoops. You'd think it would be easier to keep invisible hoops of energy circling than with real ones, but it's not. The mind wanders to laundry or a grocery list, some past upset or future concern. You drop the hoops, pick them up, get them going again. But, in qigong as with hooping, you can't *try* to flow. The only way to sustain it is to hand over in a way, like a boat riding a river. At the end of practice, as always, I stand eyes closed, hands over my belly, breathing. If the practice is a journey, this is its destination: to simply stand here breathing, allowing everything to integrate. In the stillness, the sensation of "qi"—the subtle, life-force energy—becomes most palpable. Like a dancing within.

After practice I feel none the wiser about my Nola story but happily, no longer care. Walking around the apartment looking for remnant souvenirs, I find a spoon rest decorated with a cartoon image of Decatur Street; a well-used pot holder with a recipe on it for bread pudding and whiskey sauce; the green silk flower that the fellow who rode the toy horse on the St. Charles Streetcar gave me when I saw him again on the #11 bus down Magazine after my farewell with Casey. Turning the green silk flower in my fingers it occurs to me that, while it's not a tangible thing, my favorite souvenir is the sense memory of standing on Constance Street, especially that last August evening, holding my palms to the warm brick wall. Nine years later, still with me, like it holds everything of the journey that came before. What was that phrase on the wall at the Ogden Museum of Southern Art, the day I went to see the exhibit of Eudora Welty's photographs?

". . . both a geographic location, and a state of mind."

The green silk flower stops turning in my fingers. I stare at it. I get my Nola story off the shelf, read it again.

You can go to Constance Street, between Julia and Saint Joseph. You'll see the back side of a hotel, a gravel parking lot. I think you'll see, as I first did, nothing of note. Just a place to stand and swelter in the summer heat. In August, bugs crawling the walls of the hotel. Crazy ants swarming the cracks in the sidewalk. Maybe a little lizard. Maybe a person or two shuffling by. If you look up, above the street, behind a wall, is my windowless white room. If you stand there for a day or two or a month or four, you might wander down the street to what used to be the blue side doors of the Children's Museum, if they're still there, feel something in the bricks when you put your hands to them. Maybe, remnant heat from the day. Maybe, something more.

Or, more likely, you might find yourself on another street, somewhere else in New Orleans, or somewhere else entirely, where you suddenly feel yourself stilled and complete, not wanting to be anywhere else in the world. It may not be a forest, an ocean outlook, a desert, or anywhere natural and obvious like that. It may be a location easily overlooked and walked by, a place you least expect to find grace. Like on Constance, between Julia and Saint Joseph. It will be there waiting for you. You will have to leave and move on, but I wish you that moment. And that you carry it with you.